Have you ever wondered why you just don't "click" with some people? Jon and Mindy Hirst have masterfully distilled a complicated subject and made it understandable. They help us see that there are various ways to view truth and that how we approach it dramatically impacts our lives and relationships. With biblical references and practical examples they encourage us on the journey toward truth partnered with love. Prepare your heart and mind for new understanding as you read.

Shelly Volkhardt
Missionary and Speaker
Author, *Holy Habits* and *Kitchen Table Counseling*

Through the River is a welcome synthesis of perspectives on truth, adapted from Paul Hiebert's groundbreaking *Missiological Implications of Epistemological Shifts*. Humans tend to be creatures of extremes, and one of the many illustrations of this is the antithesis of positivism (the modernist end of the spectrum of truth) and instrumentalism (the postmodernist end of the spectrum). Jon and Mindy Hirst offer a middle way that ably utilizes the strengths of both camps while tempering their weaknesses. This book persuasively conveys the truthful humility and balance of critical realism, and argues that the discovery and holistic implementation of biblical truth takes place in the context of an interdependent community.

Kenneth Boa
PhD, New York University and DPhil, Oxford
President, Reflections Ministries, Atlanta, GA

Jon and Mindy Hirst have performed an outstanding service for the church at large by making the crucial issue of epistemology (the science of knowing) clear and practical. Basing their work on the late Paul Hiebert's groundbreaking book on this subject, they have constructed an analogy that readers will easily grasp and appreciate. Christians wondering how to deal with critical challenges to their faith will find this book an invaluable tool for understanding how they themselves and others look at the world and their own lives.

Jim Reapsome
Founding Editor, *Evangelical Missions Quarterly*

Questions about "the truth" and how we can know it have exercised the greatest theological and philosophical minds of the West for the past 500 years. In a diverse, pluralistic society, Christians can sometimes cling to false certainties or be tempted to defend their faith on existential grounds (i.e. "it works for me"). Jon and Mindy Hirst guide us beyond these false alternatives to a third position, in which "true truth" exists but our understanding of it is flawed and provisional, given that we see "in a glass darkly." I believe this book will help us to think more clearly about how we testify with bold humility to the truth of God as revealed in his Son Jesus Christ.

Richard Tiplady
British Director, European Christian Mission
Author, *One World or Many?: The Impact of Globalisation on Mission*

Through the River

UNDERSTANDING
YOUR ASSUMPTIONS
ABOUT TRUTH

Jon & Mindy Hirst
WITH Dr. Paul Hiebert

Authentic

COLORADO SPRINGS · MILTON KEYNES · HYDERABAD

Authentic Publishing
We welcome your questions and comments.

USA   1820 Jet Stream Drive, Colorado Springs, CO 80921
      www.authenticbooks.com
UK   9 Holdom Avenue, Bletchley, Milton Keynes, Bucks, MK1 1QR
      www.authenticmedia.co.uk
India Logos Bhavan, Medchal Road, Jeedimetla Village, Secunderabad
      500 055, A.P.

Through the River
ISBN 13: 978-1-934068-03-8

Cover design: Nick Lee
Interior design: projectluz.com
Editorial team: Bette Smyth, Michaela Dodd, John Dunham

Printed in the United States of America

CONTENTS

FOREWORD

In a session for pastors at the Urbana 2006 Student Missions Convention, Rick Warren was asked a question about his decision to involve then-Senator Barack Obama in his 2006 Saddleback Church HIV/AIDS conference. The question implied condemnation toward Rick for allowing someone to speak whose Democratic party advocated a "pro-choice" approach to abortion rather than the traditional "pro-life" platform of evangelical Christians.

Rick responded graciously and started by articulating his own very strong "pro-life" convictions, but he went on to explain that Senator Obama was invited—along with conservative Republican Senator Sam Brownback—to speak about their commitment to battling HIV/AIDS, and *not* about the abortion issue. Then Rick summarized: *"If we are willing to work only with people who believe as we do on every point, we will find ourselves alone."*

Rick's comment reflected what may be the greatest challenge facing Christians today: *engagement*. What does it mean to be "salt" and "light" in the world? How do we engage the cultures in which we live in order to communicate the Gospel in both word and deed? Can I defend the rights of the unborn and yet engage in civil conversation—and even learn from—those with whom I disagree? How do I affirm truth if my culture prefers postmodern relativism?

The challenge of engagement permeates our daily lives. How do I talk to my Hindu neighbor about Christ? What do I tell my son when he observes that the Mormon kids at school are more moral than the kids who call themselves Christians? What do I say to that co-worker who believes that truth is totally subjective? And even in my church, how can I encourage one Christian to understand that another Christian (who is truly Christian) voted for the other political party for different reasons?

At the core of this challenge is what Jon and Mindy Hirst refer to as the "truth lens." As you'll read in the pages that follow, our truth lens affects every aspect of our lives. It affects values, ethics, relationships, the way we communicate, decision-making, and our ability to build bridges in the culture or cultures we're endeavoring to reach.

Facing the truth lens challenge (i.e., relating to people who see the world differently) is never easy. Some resort to the "my way or the highway" approach, insisting on relating to (and often worshipping with) only those who rigidly believe the way they believe on every point—including points that others might consider minor or insignificant. As the Hirsts explain, these people manage to survive in the world by keeping their convictions about truth separated from daily life in lifestyle silos (read on!).

Others react to such rigidity, and they throw in the towel of truth in favor of a "whatever" approach to truth. There is no truth; there is only "truth for me." Like the pastor who ended his sermons with a non-committal, "But then again, what do I know?" these move in the direction that humorist Bill Cosby referred to as "so open minded their brains fall out." Concepts of absolute truth get buried in accusations of intolerance and bigotry.

The Hirsts introduce us to a better way, a way that allows us to affirm "the truth we know as well as the truth we are learning" (and I might add "un-learning") through life, relationships, experiences, and active engagement with our culture. Get ready to read a book that will get you to think about the ways that we think. Scholars call this epistemology, but the Hirsts make the concept much easier to understand than something that requires a six-syllable word!

This book will strengthen your own discipline of thinking and forming convictions based on theological truth that the Bible affirms, but it will also expand your desire to understand and learn from others. In short, it will provide a perspective on a truth lens that will help you engage in the postmodern, multi-cultural world in which we live.

For me personally, the Hirst's teaching on "critical realism" (read on to understand what this is) helps me understand my culture—gleaning from the insights of others who do not necessarily subscribe to my convictions about truth. It gives me a better idea of how to engage people of other world religions in meaningful conversations. It even helps me gain perspective on the disagreements between Christians who conflict because of their various generationally-influenced and/or experience-oriented truth lenses. And most importantly, the teaching on critical real-ism helps expand my understanding of Lord Jesus, who promised that his truth will make us free. Let me explain.

In a meeting with African leaders in Addis Ababa, Ethiopia, my Ugandan host and I got into a heavy theological discussion/debate about ancestors and the phrase in Hebrews 12 about being "surrounded by a great cloud of witnesses." My Western, scientific-influenced worldview thought of these people as inspir-ing historical characters of the past. His African, connected-to-the-past worldview thought of them as mysteriously somehow actually present to encourage us. We disagreed, but as we walked toward our next meeting, he turned and said, "We must have these conversa-tions, for if we do not, we will each end up with our own village God."

We both agreed. Our truth lenses were influenced by the cultures and contexts from which we had come. But by dialogue together, we could affirm the truth we know and discover truth we are learning by each other's perspectives. The end result: an understanding of a God who is greater than either of us had previ-ously understood.

My prayer is that this book expands your mind about the ways that we think—in order to expand your understanding of the God of all truth.

Dr. Paul Borthwick

LESSONS AT THE WATER'S EDGE

ater. Every moment of our lives is affected by this wet, sparkling substance. We crave it when we're thirsty, we submerge ourselves in it when we bathe, and we choose our homes near its sources. We are made up of water at the cellular level, as it permeates our very existence and defines our lives. Sustaining and refreshing, water is so essential to life that when we search for life on other planets, one of the most important questions we ask is whether the planet has water.

When water is in motion, its power is breathtaking, not simply in its beauty but in its motion, its personality, and its decisive force. Many people feel a sense of connection with rivers. Some are large and broad, wandering leisurely through landscapes; others cut the land like jagged knives, running foamily over dirt and rocks. Others decorate the land like shining ribbons woven through the green. As the rivers of this world gurgle and weave, they often run through our lives in memorable ways. Rivers have always been forces of nature that separate countries, feed people, and impact environments.

Think back to some of the rivers in your past. As for us—Jon and Mindy—rivers have punctuated our lives in significant ways. In fact, rivers had been a part of our lives long before we knew each other. And just as rivers merge and become one, when we met, our river experiences merged and are now a shared influence in our lives.

Jon thinks of one riverbank seeping with moisture, the steam still rising from the early morning waters. He remembers sitting next to his grandfather and hoping for a bite on that limp bit of string. He saw many fish that day, and even though he didn't catch a single one, he learned a lesson about expectations.

Once, Mindy went canoeing with a youth group. The canoe flipped near the rapids and filled with water, jamming itself against the rocks and pinning her leg. She had to ask for help from a canoe of smirking friends sliding past. That day she learned about humility and survival.

Jon remembers facing down another river when he was a small child. The water was rushing beneath his feet, and all he had for a bridge was a thin log. As he slowly inched along, he learned about courage.

Mindy remembers grasping a yellow rubber raft racing down a swollen midwestern river in early spring. A frightened little sister sat atop the overturned flotation device while another sister held on tightly next to her, half-frightened, half-elated at the adventure. That day she learned a lesson about responsibility for others and the fragility of life.

When Jon went away to college, a creek covered in a leafy green canopy slid silently past his dorm room. During the rainy season it became a muddy adventure. So with a small rubber raft and a good friend, he defied the college dean's warning and rafted down the river—only to get caught on the second try. That day he learned about risk and consequences.

A few years later on our honeymoon, we spent a week in a cabin on another midwestern river. We hiked, canoed, and picnicked by that river, and we learned about love. Several months later, as we were considering our path together, we read *A Severe Mercy* by Sheldon VanAuken, sitting by the very creek where our lives first merged. There we decided to go on mission together and serve God with our careers.

As we look back, each of these river experiences defined our lives in a new and wonderful way—propelling us forward in our growth, relationships, and careers. And now the river has become an appropriate analogy in the search for truth that we are about to share with you.

Now some of you are picking this book up because you see it draws heavily on the work of Dr. Paul Hiebert. For those of you who have known him or known of him, we hope you will enjoy this very different approach to his ideas. But don't expect an academic book as he would have written. If you are looking for that, read the relevant text he wrote, *Missiological Implications of Epistemological Shifts: Affirming Truth in a Modern/Postmodern World*.[1] As you read this book, you will see many quotes and citations from his important work. While working with Dr. Hiebert, we developed this different approach with the goal of challenging you, the reader, to think about these concepts as they apply to your daily life and relationships. Throughout the process, we desired to carefully draw from the scriptural and missiological foundation on which he built his work.

Dr. Hiebert, who passed away in the spring of 2007, was one of the most influential missions thinkers in the twentieth century. Much of his life's work was directed toward how we use anthropology in our Great Commission cause. His writings and teachings have propelled many into missions and into lovingly working with those who desperately need Christ.

Paul Hiebert was a missionary kid born in India in 1932. He returned to India to be a missionary for six years before he accepted a series of teaching positions, including Kansas State, University of Washington, Fuller Seminary, and finally Trinity Evangelical Divinity School. A prolific writer, he wrote over twelve books and published over one hundred fifty articles. For more on his life, his scholarship, and his passion for missions visit: www. throughtheriverbook.com.

We were warmly welcomed into Dr. Hiebert's kitchen one June day and were surrounded by trinkets representing his many years in India and his travels around the world. We heard his passion to help people understand how they think and how to effectively reach out in relationship to those in other cultures.

He represented what we call a *generous mind*—someone who takes what God has given and shares it with others. In fact, our entry into this project is very much a result of his generosity.

When we first read his work, the ideas excited us, and we immediately wanted to see his audience expanded. When Jon went to visit him to suggest he write another book recasting his main ideas, he told Jon, "You should do it!"

Thus began our relationship with Dr. Hiebert and with the topic he has raised. The more we digested the concepts, the more we became convinced that this topic is truly life changing. It is a component to understanding many forces at work today—rules, manipulation, irrelevance, irrational tolerance, and the list goes on.

We hope you hear the voice of Dr. Hiebert calling out through these pages. But more important than his voice, our hope is that you hear God's voice speaking to you through these ideas. Our prayer is nothing less than life transformation for every reader. That might sound bold, but we pray these concepts will impact every area of your life and change the way you look at relationships.

So whether you are very familiar with Dr. Hiebert's writing or whether those last few paragraphs were your first introduction, we hope that you will enjoy our practical and simple approach to his original work.

We hope you enjoy this journey through the river.

ACKNOWLEDGEMENTS

O n a journey you meet many people. There are countless engaging conversations, compelling stories, and powerful visions. So it is that on our journey we have many people to thank for their generous minds.

Dr. Paul Hiebert: We are indebted to this wonderful man for his ideas, his friendship, and his courage. He believed in us, two young thinkers, enough to share his ideas and release them to us as we began to write this book. We miss him deeply, as he is now in the presence of his Lord.

Les and Priscilla Hirst: Jon's parents and our dear friends are the ones who introduced us to Dr. Hiebert's ideas and to the man himself. They provided an invaluable sounding board throughout the entire process of writing this book. At every step they have encouraged and facilitated our vision. Thank you!

Jim Reapsome: Through Jim's patient editing and encouragement, he launched Jon's writing efforts as his mentor in college. He had confidence in us and introduced us to Authentic Publishers.

We would like to thank our family and friends who loved us through our journeys and continue to stand beside us. We especially thank our three wonderful children—Isa, Adin, and Emi—who gave up significant "Mom and Dad time" so we could write this book.

Chapter 1

THREE COMMUNITIES ALONG THE RIVER

Have you ever wondered why so many discussions turn into arguments? Or why your most cherished relationships often strain under the pressure of who is right and who is wrong? In our quest for understanding truth and finding peace in relationships, we found a voice of hope and a way ahead in Paul Hiebert's book *Missiological Implications of Epistemological Shifts: Affirming Truth in a Modern/Postmodern World*. We felt his message needed to be taken to those outside his core audience. So we met with Dr. Hiebert to develop our approach to present his innovative ideas in an entirely new way, while keeping the biblical foundation.

It is important to understand that the core information we will go through is explained more thoroughly in Dr. Hiebert's work. We have taken his concepts one step further to build helpful analogies, point to the Scripture, and make suggestions on how these ideas apply to our lives and relationships. We have done our best to make notations when we are paraphrasing and to use quotations when appropriate so that it is clear which concepts we learned from Dr. Hiebert and when we have gone on to apply those ideas. However, this book truly was a joint effort, and those lines get fuzzy in places. We owe a great deal to Dr. Hiebert for his investment in us.

River Town

Understanding truth is a lifelong process, but where do you start? One of the most helpful analogies Hiebert introduced to us is that of the river.[1] So we begin our journey in a town built along a river. The people of River Town will offer insights into the struggles we face in life as we try to understand truth and relationships.

In this small town in the countryside, the people live simply. They are smart, friendly, warm, and value relationships with those around them. But there is conflict in the town. There are three communities, and whenever they try to communicate, the messages seem to get lost in the air between them.

The three communities are impacted by a river running through the middle of the town, which cuts the terrain into two very different landscapes. On one side the ground is solid with large rocky mounds rising from a pebbly beach, and the other side has meadows gently swelling into the mountains. The river itself is wide and is dotted with sandy islands.

The lives of the Rock Dwellers are independent and controlled. Their houses are carefully planned and each is built on a separate mound, with the boundaries clearly delineated. Each person has firmly held beliefs, and although they may not come to the same conclusions, they agree on the rules for finding solutions, believing there is one right answer to every problem. Using these rules based on reason and logic, they try to come to a consensus of a single correct position. Entertainment often centers on spirited debates and oratory. From their mounds they deliver great speeches, argue the finer points of the issue at hand, and go to sleep each evening in glorious victory or sullen defeat. There is a hint of distrust among the people, since certainty is so important and every debate creates a doubt or an ambiguity.

The river laps against the pebbly beach. When wading out into the water, you need to watch your step as the shallow water suddenly grows deep, and you could slip on the wet pebbles and find yourself submerged. The Rock Dwellers prefer to stay out of the water. They warn their children of the dangers of the shifting sand. They tell stories of relatives who have waded into the water and were never quite the same.

If you swim through the deep water, you will surely meet the people who make the river their home—the Island Dwellers. They settled where the water becomes shallow again, banking into sandbars where marshy beaches make patterns down the stream. Some of these sandbars have managed to grow small trees, but these islands are only temporary structures at the mercy of the weather and the river's changing moods. The Island Dwellers spend their days in and around the water, enjoying a life of drifting. They are friendly people who love to talk and discuss the beauty of their world. They rarely argue, as their nonconfrontational life is more important to them than seeing eye to eye. Many of them have come from the rocky terrain to live in the river, preferring the mild acceptance of the Island Dwellers. But their connections to each other are as fleeting as the sandy dunes they live on.

Their homes are on the myriad of small islands that give contour to the river's constant current. Each island is a beautiful home for a family to live in and love each other. However, the greatest challenge for them is that there are no bridges. Each island sits separated from the others. The families all know of other people living in the river's flow but think, "How much could we really have in common?" Each island is a separate reality, with individual experiences of joy and pain.

Continuing across the river, the water runs muddy and deep. Near the shore a jungle of rushes and plant life make it difficult to navigate or swim. As you come out of the water, the scene is striking. There is a beautiful valley of green grasses and lush trees. If you follow the valley's rolling contours, your gaze begins to rise with the land. Soon you are feasting on a forest of pine with grey peaks jutting out in the glistening sun.

On this far shore, the Valley Dwellers build their houses close together. Each person has a separate space, but the design of the settlement indicates that communication is important. Here there is a sense of sharing and community. The village has a common courtyard where the people come together to tell stories and discuss ideas in a posture of learning and growing. People are excited to hear from each other because they believe that every person brings a new perspective.

The Valley Dwellers are hikers and foresters. They spend their free time venturing from the valley into the forests and mountain meadows above. From each trip they return to share what they have seen, what they have learned, and how it has changed them. This community is growing, as some of the Rock and Island Dwellers have come across to live among them. Even now, a young man is coming out of the river and someone is giving him a hand onto the grassy shore. He is out of breath. It has been a tough swim, but the man is smiling at the effort.

The Importance of Your Truth Lens

River Town gives us a mental picture of how communities can live in proximity while looking at the world in totally different ways. These three groups live and act so differently because each group has different assumptions about truth. These assumptions include how they view the world, how they interpret the discoveries they make, and how they live in relationship with others who are making their own discoveries.

The way we each look at life's great issues is so basic that it is hard to even think about. It impacts every aspect of life in modern culture. Our worldviews are formed in the first years of life, and they provide the basis for how we understand and deal with reality.[2] Even though our worldview figures in every decision we make, it is not easily observable or accessible to us. Hiebert described it this way: "Like the glasses we wear, we find it harder to see our own worldview than others looking at us."[3]

Every worldview—and there are many out there—has an epistemology built into it. The word *epistemology* means the study of the nature and origins of knowledge.[4] This does not mean that each of us studies knowledge, but it does mean that each of us has a unique way of processing knowledge and internalizing beliefs. Our epistemological underpinnings are subtle, and, for that reason, they can be taken for granted or even dismissed as philosophical wonderings.

We might think of an epistemology as a *truth lens* because it serves much like the glasses that Hiebert described above when he spoke of a worldview. Our epistemologies sit like glasses perched on the bridges of our noses, helping us to evaluate the daily influx of situations and information. We call these epistemologies truth lenses throughout the book to help us remember the role this tool plays in our thinking.

Simply put, truth lenses are your assumptions about truth. They define how you think about what you know. These assumptions are what you believe is the truth *about* truth. There are varied assumptions about truth: you might believe that truth is completely knowable or that it is only knowable by you or that it is out there waiting to be discovered. It is these assumptions about what we can know that drive many of our daily decisions.

These truth lenses are the things you think with, internal tools the brain uses to organize the world, like our worldview, culture, and experiences.[5] They are part of the foundation on which we build our thinking. It is not easy to think about these tools, since we're always using them. In his book *Studies in Words*, C. S. Lewis said that "prolonged thought *about* the words which we ordinarily use to *think with* can produce a momentary aphasia."[6] Thinking about our epistemologies may also cause a sort of thought-speechlessness when we look at them directly to understand how we make sense of the world. But it is worth the process, and Lewis said of this aphasia in the context of understanding words, "I think it is to be welcomed."[7]

Our truth lens forms a basic foundation that allows us to order our world and define our reality. Our truth lens deeply affects how we live and relate with those around us. In fact, our truth lens will influence whether we tell others about what we know, insist that they accept what we know, or be resigned to keep what we know to ourselves.

Though there are more, we will focus on three truth lenses and represent them in the River Town analogy. Each community represents a different truth lens: the Rock Dwellers on the rocky shore are using the truth lens of *positivism*; the Island Dwellers on the sandbars are using the truth lens of *instrumentalism*; and the Valley Dwellers on the far shore are using the truth lens of *critical realism*. The truth lenses of all three groups are based in realism—believing in a real, external world that exists outside of the mind.[8] However, there are some significant differences in what they believe about understanding that world. By interacting with these three communities within River Town, we can reflect on and begin to understand this very important part of our worldviews.

Our truth lens impacts how we relate with others. How many times have we gotten into the car after a social event, shaking our heads and wondering what went wrong—again? The answer to the question, What do we think with? could begin to shine light into that troubling moment in the car. By discovering what we and others think with, we find that many of the challenges we have in relationships are rooted in differences in our truth lenses. As we begin to understand how people relate based on what they believe about truth, we become more informed about how we relate in our most important relationships. We also begin to see how our views of truth affect and inform other decisions we make.

This discovery of what we think with and our assumptions about truth, if understood in the light of the Bible, can begin to change our relationships, our worldviews, and even our values and attitudes. As you walk through this journey with us, take some time to pray that God will help you see if the assumptions you use every day line up with the Bible.

Truth's Hard Questions

On an average day filled with errands, work, and family, we don't have the time to ask the hard questions about truth. But for people of faith, understanding truth and what we believe about it is an important foundational step to building a biblical view of the world. Questions like, Is my view of truth in line with the Bible? or How does the way I view truth affect my faith, my relationships, and my work? are good beginning questions.

Because of the significance of the topic, there is plenty of controversy. There are those who feel a loss of simple truth, those who consider truth to be overrated, those who feel confident in the truth they know, and those searching for a way to understand truth when the circumstances of life seem to neutralize it.

The handling of truth in a new millennium brings many opinions and many concerns. This wildfire is being stoked by a global economy that trades in ideas that are sold as truth. Many of us feel overwhelmed by it all as we see our friends, children, spouses, or coworkers lost in a world where ideas of all kinds are presented as truth. Others of us live confident of truth and confront those who disagree with us with similar confidence. Still others are trying to see truth through a different truth lens.

The confusion is great, but the stakes are even greater. Our worldviews, and specifically our truth lenses, are the building blocks necessary to construct bridges that can span the gaps between people, representing the passion of Christ to a hurting world. Unless our worldviews (and within that, our truth lenses) are centered on God's perspective, we cannot share hope with people of different cultures, points of view, and ways of life.

In fact, our ability to struggle through the concept of truth in today's world is crucial to determining our success in the Christian life, our relationships, and our kingdom work.

Truth's Foundation

As we journey, we are striving to understand the lens by which we view truth and how that view impacts us practically. To do that, we need to have a common definition of truth that will connect with the Bible's teaching.

First, let's think about some definitions of truth. The *American Heritage Dictionary* describes truth as "conformity to fact or actuality; a statement proven to be or accepted as true; sincerity; integrity." Different people react to the concept of truth in very different ways. Herman Melville said, "Truth is the silliest thing under the sun. Try to get a living by the Truth—and go to the Soup Societies. Heavens!"[9] Thomas Jefferson affirmed truth but made some distinctions as he strove to be culturally relevant yet morally bound: "In matters of style, swim with the current; in matters of principle, stand like a rock."[10] Winston Churchill acknowledged the elusiveness of truth when he said, "Men occasionally stumble over the truth, but most of them pick themselves up and hurry off as if nothing ever happened."[11] When it comes to truth, most people have a fuzzy concept of what it means, and stumble over how to deal with it.

So what is truth at its most basic level? Simply put, we know that God is truth. He is the Creator of all that is sure, all that is known, and all that is to be. In Isaiah 48:17 the prophet presented this God of truth: "This is what the LORD says—your Redeemer, the Holy One of Israel: 'I am the LORD your God, who teaches you what is best for you, who directs you in the way you should go.'" By establishing God's lordship, Isaiah's prophecy is placing authority in God's reign and placing all of our pursuits under that authority. All that we want to know and all that we hope to learn is within the context of God's power.

Then as Jesus came to earth and established a beachhead for the kingdom of God, he reiterated what was said in Isaiah in John 14:6: "Jesus answered, 'I am the way and the truth and the life. No one comes to the Father except through me.'" The amazing thing is that he went one step further than Isaiah. Isaiah spoke of the "what is best," but Jesus spoke of "the way." There is no doubt that Jesus is all that we need to know in order to have life.

Our pursuit of truth may begin in ourselves, as we struggle with our finite humanity, but it ends in Christ. All of the things that we want to know are discovered as we develop our relationship with him. So as we turn now to exploring these three truth lenses, let's base that exploration on what we know of God and ask him to give us wisdom as we seek to learn more about how we approach truth.

Chapter 2

THE RIVER TOWN STORY

The story of the Rock Dwellers, Island Dwellers, and Valley Dwellers is the tale of three truth lenses that dominate our society today. There are many more than three in our world, but our story will focus on these three ways of looking at truth.

One commonality among all three of the communities along the river is that they believe in a form of realism. Realism is the basis for all three truth lenses in River Town; therefore, we'll start there in order to understand how each community thinks. Realism holds that there is an objective reality independent of people's perceptions of it. So as you get to know the three communities, keep in mind that they all want to know what is real and experience it; but they have different assumptions about that reality.

Understanding the Three Truth Lenses

The Rock Dwellers are positivists. The term *positivism* was first developed by August Comte, and it describes the view that through empirical methods and observation, we can discover the laws that govern our world.[1] Positivism proposes that all truth about us and our world is knowable and that it is our job to engage in an active search for that truth, allowing us to expose untruth.

Positivism sounds like a strange concept, but it is easy to remember if you think about some basic math. After all, math is the *lingua franca* of positivism, because its search is for things that are completely and objectively knowable. Think about truth as a process of addition and subtraction. When discovering truth, the process is similar to addition. Knowledge and truth are added to experience. At the same time, untruth is being discovered and subtracted from that experience. A person with the positivist truth lens is focused on adding truth and subtracting untruth every day.

In our River Town analogy, we find that this positivist truth lens did not satisfy everyone in the initial settlement on the rocky shore. There were some who believed that there was a whole set of knowledge—such as personal perspective, culture, and perception—being ignored in the pursuit of objectivity. These people left the rocky shore and became the Island Dwellers.

Life in the river as Island Dwellers meant no longer having to reject personal perspective and feelings in the pursuit of truth. Instead, they embraced each individual's viewpoint, believing that even though there is a real world outside of what we think, our understanding of that world is unique. No one can accurately understand the world of another, because our understanding rests in our minds and is affected by personal experience, culture, and thought. Objective language cannot truly be objective because people create it. This truth lens is known as *instrumentalism* and it makes the river a comfortable place to live without judgment or the need to prove what is right.

The swift currents of thought in this river of instrumentalism drew some people away from the rocky shore by providing a way to factor culture and social dynamics into decisions about truth. While Island Dwellers believe that there is a real, external world that they can touch and feel, their main contention is that truth about this external world is a cultural creation.

The instrumentalist truth lens is completely personalized—the niche community or culture creates it—and Island Dwellers do not see a need to make truth consistent to anyone outside of themselves. As this truth lens allows for reality to be individualized, the mind becomes the playground—whereas the physical world is the playground of the person wearing the truth lens of positivism.

As people are exposed to numerous hypotheses about global problems, many give up believing that universal truth exists. Instead, they look at ideas very pragmatically, using the ones that work and leaving the others alone. In doing this they allow their conclusions to be their own, whether or not their friends, their families, or their professors agree. As long as it works, it is true enough.

The danger of instrumentalism is that it can lead to hopelessness. People may conclude life is meaningless because there is no common truth to build on. This reality is magnified by the many cultures people are exposed to in our global society. As wave after wave of ideas from different cultures flood people's lives, many decide that their definitions of truth do not have to align with those from other parts of the world in order to be valid. In essence, instrumentalists believe that it is impossible to systematize the myriad ideas of reality to make them relevant and useful to all.

As a result, instrumentalists believe that any lifestyle is acceptable. Tolerance of many religions and spiritual practices flourish as people experiment with what would best suit their personal needs. In his book *In Search for Certainty*, John Guest described it this way, "What you perceive in your mind in the first place is totally subjective; you then take that subjective personal view and describe it in words; those words are communicated to another mind which not only has a totally different understanding of the words but hears them in the context of a totally different life experience."[2]

So, while the Island Dwellers loved their lifestyle, something was missing. They had no foundation on which to build their lives and make decisions. They felt alone and disconnected. Many had no desire to leave the islands, but a few sensed that there must be a better way to live. They could either return to the rocky shore or they could push on and see what the other shore was like. Some did go back, but a small group pushed ahead into the unknown.

They ventured forward because of their desire for a solution that would satisfy both their need for a foundation and their desire for true connections. The extreme isolation of the islands left a void because people are intrinsically designed for community. And out of this void came the third truth lens that we will be considering— the truth lens of *critical realism*. We will see that it is a harmonizing of the two previous truth lenses. Critical realism understands that foundational truths about our world and humanity must exist. At the same time, it realizes that our world houses billions of people with countless perspectives on what those truths look like. The key is that it allows for a learning process in which foundational truths exist and can be discovered in community. Truth about our external world is first understood internally. But we are not left all alone in a world inside our minds. Instead, critical realism encourages us to interact with others to better understand their perceptions, as we seek to gain a fuller understanding of truth.

Critical realism offers a hopeful view of truth that allows for personal interpretation, while believing that we can understand each other. This understanding allows us to grow in our knowledge of the world by working together to share what we know. This truth lens encourages people to understand cultures and through this understanding to see what truths can be discovered. It also places value on history and narrative, finding meaning through context. It recognizes the significant interdependence in our world that forces us to understand each other and define the things that we have in common.

In a Christian's search for truth, critical realism promotes a search for the core truths of the Bible that are discovered through the many different perspectives of people growing in their faith around the world. We like to describe this truth lens as *the truth we know and the truth we are learning.*

The *truth we know* is those foundational beliefs that guide our lives. For Christians this is the Bible and the character of God. It may include belief in scientific discovery, and it will also include belief in spiritual activities. Some aspects of positivism (the belief that absolute truth exists) and of instrumentalism (the belief that truth is individually perceived) are also included.

The *truth we are learning* is those things that are not completely known, which we learn by thinking and interacting with others in our search for truth. This is where learning from other cultures becomes important to discovering our world. As Hiebert explained, "Different cultures ask different questions."[3] It is through finding answers to these new questions that we have a more complete understanding of any subject.

In River Town the life of a Valley Dweller is in many ways a different experience from the life of a Rock Dweller and an Island Dweller. Critical realism gives Valley Dwellers the hope of truly knowing the world (an idea they lost in the river of instrumentalism) without the impossible task of divorcing their feelings and perspectives from what they know (a daily exercise on the shore of positivism). Living in community with others brings joy to the Valley Dwellers.

In 1 Corinthians 13 the apostle Paul wrote that now we "see through a glass, darkly" (v. 12, KJV). Critical realism can endure and even embrace this sense of mystery and uncertainty because knowledge is a process and there is a hope of seeing "face to face" in eternity. This truth lens provides a strong sense of community because it assures us that we are all on a journey of knowing together.

Ripples of Influence

In order to understand the truth lenses that people think with today, it's important to grasp the main influences that have shaped them. Truth lenses change over time, and one lens does not displace another completely. Imagine a still pond whose surface is unbroken. Throw a pebble into that pond, and the impact begins to ripple, affecting the entire surface. Throw a second and a third pebble, and you will see how the effects are completely interrelated. Ripples overlap with other ripples, and the entire surface is dynamic.

The experience of the history of truth lenses is much like floating on the surface of that pond. Wherever you are on the surface, you are affected by one or all of the ripples caused by those pebbles. So it is less like a chronological experience in which a new lens replaces an old one at the turn of a century, but more like a process in which the thoughts of key individuals affect the thinking of larger and larger groups of people over time.

There are many people throwing pebbles into the pond. It's not as simple as three interacting circles of waves, but a whole world of people throwing in their ideas to create waves of thinking.

There are some key individuals whose ideas impact the ways we think today. They may have thrown their pebble in the pond long ago, but the ripples of their thoughts still affect us

Influence of Plato

Centuries before Christ's birth, Greek thought began to influence many cultures to take a less holistic, more analytical approach. Plato suggested a significant shift in thinking about truth when he stated that the real world was not one integrated whole, but was divided into two very distinct categories.[4] With the separation of the material and spiritual worlds, secularism was born.

When the once-firm foundation of realism became influenced by Greek thought, narrative began to lose its importance. As story receded, questions about the nature of reality took a larger role in people's thinking. This motivated them to discuss and argue their theories until one was proven and accepted as truth in their community.

With the birth of secular thought came many of the fields of study we have today. The scientific method became prominent, with its focus on objectivity as the basis for discovering the material world. The emerging disciplines of science, sociology, and mathematics became central to Western culture. As this occurred the world became increasingly crowded with information, making the older truth lenses more cumbersome to use when making practical decisions.

Influence of Copernicus

Another influencer was Nicholas Copernicus who proposed that the earth revolves around the sun. Previously, the world had developed an explanation for the sun's movement. Based on simple observation, people believed that the sun circled around the earth. And because physical realities and spiritual realities were viewed holistically at that time, the church used this physical reality to make a spiritual point—God made this earth special, with humanity as the center of the wider universe.

Then along came Copernicus. He questioned this view of the world and began looking for the systems of truth that would explain not only the sun's movement, but the movements of all celestial objects. He made new observations and calculations, and it led him to announce that the earth moved around the sun—contradicting centuries of thought.[5] Through his studies he was adding truth to the conversation and subtracting untruth. Copernicus's ideas clashed with long-held ideas about the universe. "Copernicus lived and worked during a period when rapid changes in political, economic, and intellectual life were preparing the bases of modern European and American civilization. His planetary theory and his associated concept of a sun-centered universe were instrumental in the transition from medieval to modern Western society, because they seemed to affect man's relation to the universe and to God."[6] And even though ancient realism temporarily won that battle, positivism was on the rise.

The clash between premodern and modern thought was messy. Civilization's reality was rocked. But out of the fray came a new reality that captured the imagination of the world. People realized that they could find solutions to problems through investigating the world, standardizing vocabulary, and adding up truth.

And so the world has spun. Stay with us as we speed through the next several hundred years of history, noting a few important signposts along the way. Positivism reigned as Europe colonized the world, as the Industrial Age brought new scientific understanding and amazing technology, and as science unlocked the human body and then the mind. Then even the outer reaches of space were brought into every home.

In many people's minds, modernity was the solution to all human troubles. People's hopes began to rise as they became convinced that with each day of adding new truth and subtracting untruth they could bring peace and justice to the world. At the same time that people were hoping to bring peace to the world, society started sounding more and more argumentative. By giving the search for truth to the individual, authority moved from the king or church to each person. This meant that there was no one person dictating truth to the masses, and people felt the responsibility to argue their cases in an objective language they all agreed on to find the one theory that was right. With the influx of so many ideas and opinions, it became more and more difficult to come to consensus on every issue.

Influence of Einstein

Many people were disillusioned because the world they thought they could know and understand would not submit to their ideas and systems. It unraveled because the utopian vision of knowing was dashed by a series of dramatic events. People's hopes for peace and justice were jarred by the First and Second World Wars. These horrific times impacted whole generations of people who saw the raw force of technology used to kill people instead of harnessing its force for progress, hope, prosperity, and—yes, truth. The truth lens of positivism was being challenged.

Whereas Copernicus exemplified the transition from realism to positivism, Albert Einstein's theory of relativity exemplified the transition from positivism to instrumentalism, though not because he intended this or believed it himself. His concept of relative space resonated with the growing idea that our understanding of truth does not have to be based on a common platform.[7] Einstein was distressed by the fact that philosophers and others applied his concepts about physics to the world of morals. While he was raised in a mix of Catholic schools and Jewish heritage, he had a strong feeling about a larger truth that could be defined. Once Einstein said, "We should take care not to make the intellect our god; it has, of course, powerful muscles, but no personality."[8]

The last half of the twentieth century was a time of rebuilding and growth that opened the doors to the global economy. Air travel and telecommunications expanded connections among people who began to experience things that they had never encountered before. They saw new religions and cultures with worldviews that brought new solutions to problems they themselves had tackled.

Over the last fifty years, many people have been living in this river of individual worlds and realities flowing unintentionally from Einstein's thinking. Truth is increasingly seen as more sub-jective and personal as science and technology speed forward with new ideas and changes to our lives and as our world shrinks around us. This truth lens doesn't try to control the increasing number of ideas, but instead allows for many ideas to exist simultaneously.

Influencers of Critical Realism

As people's experience of the world has become more individ-ualized, it has also become more global, as people are more aware of different cultures, religions, and lifestyles all over the world, not to mention within their own cities. These two great forces caused people to struggle with both positivism and instrumentalism. For the Rock Dwellers who were always adding truth and subtracting untruth, this expanded world of people and cultures exponentially increased the amount of math necessary to come to grips with their world. For the Island Dwellers, they encountered thousands more islands than they ever thought existed, but still had no bridge to any of them.

This growing challenge became more and more evident as young people returned from World War I and World War II and jumped into work, study, and life. Thomas Friedman, in his book *The World Is Flat*, suggested that along with this expanded experi-ence of the world came the rapid development of technology. He said this had a flattening effect on the world, making it critical for people to deal with the ideas and cultures of many other parts of the world in their everyday life.[9]

Just as Copernicus represents the transition to positivist thought and Einstein represents the transition to instrumentalist thought, the scientist-turned-philosopher Michael Polanyi represents the transition to critical-realist thought. Polanyi was born in Budapest in 1891 and studied medicine and physical chemistry. However, he struggled with the positivist view of knowledge promoted by most in the scientific community in which he worked. After a successful career in science, he transitioned to philosophy in the 1930s in search of a truth lens that defined truth but allowed for personal growth in that knowledge.[10]

Polanyi's experience shows the tension that began to arise in modern culture as the social sciences developed alongside the established scientific community. Sociologists opened people's minds to the reality that there is more to truth than what can be understood through the objective scientific method. Rather, they believed that to apply these methods to people is to reduce them to material objects. Out of this tension came a need for a truth lens that would allow for other ways of knowing. Hiebert explained, "In critical realism we take the ideas, feelings, values and purposes of people to be real, and seek to understand them as human beings as they reveal themselves to us. The fact that knowledge links inner worlds to outer realities makes such knowing possible. Interpersonal knowing is not simply knowledge about a person, but knowing the person intimately as fully human—as we know ourselves."[11]

More central to the development of critical realism were scholars like Charles Pierce, prior to Polanyi, and later, Ian Barbour.

These men gravitated toward critical realism because they were struggling to work in a world that required addition and subtraction. Hiebert quoted Charles Pierce who defined it well: "There are Real things, whose characters are entirely independent of our opinions about them; those Reals affect our senses according to regular laws, and, though our sensations are as different as are our relations to the objects, by taking advantage of the laws of perception, we can ascertain by reasoning how things really and truly are; and any man, if he have sufficient experience and he reason enough about it will be led to the one True conclusion."[12]

Conclusion

Now you know the story of River Town and the three communities living there. These three types of settlers have made different life decisions based on their differing truth lenses and are now living with the results of those decisions each day. Though they live independently, they are still a part of the larger community of River Town. These groups of people have chosen to live in their own communities of like-minded neighbors. Many of us experience this in our own lives. We spend much of our time with people who think like us but live in a world where we interact with people who think very differently.

You are also living out your life based on your truth lens. History has played a major part in how you think today. Perhaps by now you have a sense of which community in River Town you would be most comfortable living in. For those of you who need more time to process these truth lenses and identify where you best fit—don't stop! Something as complicated as humanity can't be put into three little neat boxes. There are many variations and infinite possibilities. The key is that you realize how important your truth lens is to your daily life and relationships.

In the next few chapters, we will engage with each of these truth lenses. We hope you will gain a new perspective in your life that will allow you to better understand your truth lens.

Chapter 3

POSITIVISM

The rocky shore was a beautiful place to settle. The breathtaking views inspired the Rock Dwellers to build homes that overlooked the shining river below. They built a town of solid structures with winding cobblestone streets and well-organized systems. Each one worked to buy the right land on which to build a home that took full advantage of the view and what the land had to offer.

The Rock Dwellers were amazed at how much progress and work could be accomplished when they all worked through the issues and found the right solutions to problems. When disagreements arose, they were able to tackle them objectively. They weren't always able to come to agreement, but they all agreed that there was a right way to think about things that could be discovered by working and debating. Finally, their community was complete when they finished their impressive town hall. Here they hoped to find consensus and solutions. Instead, as time went on, it became a place of debate.

Our world is heavily influenced by positivism, and many of you will relate to the Rock Dweller's world.

Assumptions of Positivism

Every truth lens operates from certain assumptions about truth. Though most of us spend little time thinking about these assumptions, they affect our thinking and our actions significantly—especially our understanding of the Bible and how we make practical decisions with that knowledge.

We've seen how the Rock Dwellers live: independent, driven to acquire knowledge, and proactive in dealing with inconsistencies. These traits find their roots in the assumptions of positivism. Let's take a look at some of these assumptions.

Rejecting Introspection

The positivist truth lens can best be understood as we divorce our feelings from discovery. This objectivity is deeply ingrained in modern society, and it is part of the reason relationships endure tensions produced by the search for truth. We've all heard the advice "Don't talk about religion or politics" because these topics consistently cause friction between positivists looking for the truth.

Just as personal opinion is thought to poison a quality news report, personal emotion and opinion are regarded as harmful when looking for the truth. It is *real* things that are important—those "brute sense experiences that cannot be reduced to anything else or shown to be illusions."[1] Things the mind conceives cannot be proved or disproved; therefore, they are not helpful in our search for knowledge. We should focus on the "hard reality," or "that which insists on forcing its way into human recognition as something other than the mind's creation."[2]

The scientific method is a tool to help people separate their personal feelings and perspectives from observation and experimentation in the search for knowledge. The assumption is that through empirical methods, we can find the immutable laws of nature.

This objectivity has very important results. One is that it puts the individual at the center of the truth search. In the past, authority rested in the church or experts, but in positivism, authority shifted to the individual. This is because authority in the church or of experts is rooted in culture, which is seen as subjective. In positivism only the individual is able to detach from culture in order to be objective. This movement away from traditional authority allowed for great advances in learning and innovation because the individual's mind was freed to think creatively.

Another result of this drive toward objectivity is a downplaying of culture and history in favor of timeless truth. "Science capitalizes on this freedom from context and tries to show us a contextless world, a view of things that is not affected by even that fact that it derives from our human angle of vision."[3]

While this individualism spurred on progress, it also caused people to devalue cultures that did not value science as the only way of knowing. Words like "superstitious" and "primitive" were used to describe certain cultures. So a Rock Dweller will struggle with people who see the physical and spiritual worlds as intertwined because this way of knowing cannot be truly objective and therefore cannot be accepted as fact.

Knowledge as Additive

Hiebert described the additive nature of knowledge within the positivist truth lens as building a structure: "The task of science is like erecting a building. Early scientists laid the foundations. We build on these by adding facts to the walls of knowledge. Once laid, bricks are permanent parts of the structure. Every piece of information must be accurate for the whole theory to be true. An error in any fact or deduction discredits the whole system of knowledge."[4]

Therefore Rock Dwellers feel fear when beginning to think about what they think with. Much of this fear comes from this additive assumption about knowledge. They believe that there is a danger in finding a flaw within the foundation of their thinking that will cause the whole structure to collapse. It is natural that a flood of emotion will accompany their questioning of the nature of truth.

Confidence in the Scientific Method

Based on the progress and results that positivism has brought over the last two centuries, there are some concrete reasons why it seems like a helpful truth lens. But even with all this progress, science, the active outworking of the positivist truth lens, has not delivered on its original hopes. David Harvey, a leading social theorist, said, "The scientific domination of knowledge promised freedom from scarcity, want, and the arbitrariness of natural calamity."[5] These were high hopes that looked attainable in light of the great strides of science at the time, but looking around at the world today with hunger, tragedy, and brutality, we see that science has fallen short on this promise.

The Dynamics of Dualism

Dualism is the Greek belief that the natural and supernatural worlds are completely separate. It is a core assumption of positivism. Believing that the spiritual and natural realms are separated and governed by different laws causes a Rock Dweller to keep them apart. In the extreme forms of positivism, there is the belief that the laws of science rule the material world, and there is a denial of anything spiritual. Hiebert stated, "The materialistic forms of positivism deny religious transcendence and revelation."[6]

This does not mean that a person with the positivist truth lens cannot be a Christian. Most Rock Dwellers separate their search for truth about the physical world from their search for truth in the spiritual world into different silos. They often use the same approach for both, believing that they can know the truth fully in both knowledge systems if they persevere in their efforts.

Language

One of the key challenges to the way Rock Dwellers relate to each other is the way they view words. In positivism a word has a one-to-one equivalence to reality. Feelings and personal experience are seen as stumbling blocks to transferring information clearly and to coming to objective truth. "Words were seen not as arbitrary symbols but as exact (mathematical) representations of reality—as depicting 'the way things are.'"[7]

For example, the word *tree* does not represent an imaginary tree that exists in the mind or memory, but represents an actual tree that we can touch and feel. For Rock Dwellers to be able to clearly transfer knowledge, they have to communicate the tree exactly as it is. What they think about the tree or their experiences with trees has no value. Taking personal views out of language is necessary to understanding each other and coming to the *real truth*. This one-to-one correspondence of language can cause many arguments about words and their exact meanings that deeply affect the Rock Dwellers' relationships. Math was the first language to develop that lived up to the one-to-one nature of a Rock Dweller's knowledge. Next, this concept was applied to spoken language, with scientists creating words with exact meanings to describe the world they were studying. Their intention was that people could precisely understand ideas and that everyone could come to the same conclusions. In this way, science could continue to progress and build on past discoveries. This idea assumes that all people have the ability to reason in this same way, and that if they don't, they simply are primitive and "have yet to acquire positivist knowledge. . . . Underlying this view of rationality is the assumption that there is one universal system of reason common to all humanity."[8] Culture and history are not placed into the equation, as they cloud the meaning of words.

The Picture

The positivist truth lens is building an exact picture of the world through this objectivity, exact language, and dualism. The Rock Dwellers will spend their entire lives clarifying and understanding the details of that picture. They view the world and their understanding of truth as an extremely large and complex jigsaw puzzle. They believe that all the pieces are there, waiting for discovery. Each day they play with a few of the pieces, and when one fits into place they celebrate because a bit more of that picture has become clear.

This process of filling in the picture puzzle is all consuming. Of course, this task will take many forms and will not always be a conscious activity. Every time a new idea is presented, the Rock Dwellers are compelled to take that puzzle piece and figure out where and if it fits into their puzzles.

As they are building their pictures, each Rock Dweller is exposed to some interesting interactions with others. Some are building the same picture. In these cases they build powerful connections and friendships. They work together to fill in their puzzles and will be able to share their experiences as they tackle tough problems and the truth is made clear. You probably have witnessed some of these relationships and communities today. You can see this play out in causes such as an annual pro-life event, the Humane Society, or a short-term mission trip. As people build picture puzzles together, they encourage each other and validate those discoveries as long as they agree on their findings.

During the rigor of building puzzles, Rock Dwellers encounter other views that do not connect with the picture puzzle they are building. This is one of the most difficult things for them as they try to live in community with others. They find that those who are building a similar puzzle are the exception rather than the norm, and each person who does not validate that picture causes dissonance.

Rock Dwellers have to figure out how to treat people whose ideas and beliefs do not validate the pictures they are forming. Rock Dwellers may take several different approaches:

1. They might believe that for the integrity of the picture to remain, they must reject anyone who does not agree with the picture. Rock Dwellers find themselves focusing on a small group of people of similar beliefs and perspectives.

2. They might encounter those who do not validate their picture and decide to engage them anyway. These relationships can be very positive, but they usually take two forms. Some have a playful banter of ideas with the mutual understanding that each is building separate pictures and will not be persuaded to change. Others choose to avoid those parts of the picture that are not shared and keep their friendship focused on pieces of their pictures that are the same.

3. They might also actively work to promote their picture to others. Rock Dwellers believe that others' lives will be better lived with this picture. So they take on an evangelistic approach to sharing their picture and including others in their process.

Because Rock Dwellers desire to complete their pictures, they will skeptically review all input. If most of their puzzle has blue sky, they will find themselves wary of a new idea that takes the form of purple sky. In fact, they will spend a great deal of time proving that a certain idea does not fit in their picture. Rock Dwellers will find themselves trying to prove that an idea does not fit almost as often as they are proving that it does.

One of the ways that Rock Dwellers do this is by reading and writing books, articles, and blogs that prove or disprove any given idea. They will be very interested in these because they are critical to their ability to place the next puzzle piece.

For instance, when *The Da Vinci Code* by Dan Brown came out in 2003, an idea from the Gnostic gospels was presented anew in a popular way—through a thriller novel. Immediately, the book caused dimension. It presented the idea that Jesus was married to Mary Magdalene and fathered a child whose line was being hidden from those in the church who would destroy his descendants. The book had its share of car chases, encrypted messages, and bad guys, but those were a backdrop to this big idea. If you were a positivist reading the book or hearing about it, you immediately began to sum up the content and consider whether to add it to your truth bank or subtract it as an untruth.

The Christian community acted very quickly when this book came out. Most Christians quickly put this idea in the untruth column and began to build elaborate cases for why their picture could not include this idea. Sermon series, books, speeches, and websites quickly appeared, giving reasons for why the book was untrue, for instance, titles like *Cracking the Da Vinci Code* (Catholic Answers, Inc., 2004) or *Exploring the Da Vinci Code* (Zondervan, 2006). Rock Dwellers may have been drawn to these so that they could better understand why the new idea was false, allowing them to discard that puzzle piece.

All through life there will be many *Da Vinci Code* events and the subsequent discovery processes by which Rock Dwellers decide whether or not to fit them into their puzzle. Their goal is to arrive at a completed puzzle revealing clear knowledge of the truth.

The *How* Questions

This objectivity drives the Rock Dwellers to ask the *how* questions of life. For example, How does this happen? and How can we fix it? This truth lens strives to discover the cause of events so that the outcomes can be predicted and controlled. If we can find a cure for the disease, fewer people will be sick. Positivism is most comfortable staying in this realm because the *how* is based on the basic assumption that to truly know something, it must be objective and observable. Great strides have been made asking the *how* questions. Much of the natural world can be predicted and controlled based on the answers. All around us we can see the results of the progress that positivism brings. But Hiebert warned that this thinking results in "a linear view of causality" which "leaves no place for purpose."[9]

In this way, positivism leaves out the *why* questions of life. Why are we here? and Why does disease exist? are not validated in the discovery process because positivism is more interested in finding the unchanging laws or principles that determine the one possible outcome for each event rather than finding the reasons things are the way they are. The Rock Dwellers do not think to ask about the reason or purpose behind an event that they experience.

When a person is submerged in this thinking, other ways of knowing are squeezed out of the discussion. The spiritual or moral questions are not engaged in the conversation. Hiebert noted that "naturalistic forms of positivism are intrinsically secular in nature. . . . The materialistic forms of positivism deny religious transcendence and revelation and affirm that everything is found in a single, orderly system of nature, the most fundamental realities of which are bits of material substance."[10] For the Rock Dwellers, the *why* questions of life are ignored because these cannot be discovered and tested through objective reason.

Progress

We talked about how the Rock Dwellers approach their lives as an addition and subtraction game. Hiebert described it as erecting a building, with new ideas building on the discoveries of the past. This type of thinking makes it imperative that the past ideas be correct. If one piece of the building is found to be untrue, then the whole structure is jeopardized. This plays into the fierceness with which positivists defend their views and beliefs. There is a fear that if one part of their thinking is questioned or found to be untrue, then all their beliefs must be reevaluated, or worse, rebuilt from scratch.

One result from the value positivism places on progress is that there has been an incredible explosion in knowledge. This stems from positivists' passion for knowledge and the importance placed on the individual. Think of the huge amount of energy created by this truth lens and what that energy has produced in modern society. All of the major advances in medicine, physics, and computer technology were driven by the values and systems created by positivism.

Out of these values, people using the truth lens of positivism helped birth machines. Hiebert described the values of this truth lens this way, "Rational order, control, efficiency, production and profit become primary values. The result is the commoditization and commercialization of much of life."[11] These values have made our quality of life and our global economy possible. Imagine trade between the United Kingdom and China without the smoothly efficient system of production and commerce. It would never work on a large scale. In fact, most of our daily conveniences would not work without the systems designed by Rock Dwellers. There would be no guarantee of finding potatoes in the grocery store. There would be no Internet. Cars would be an expensive luxury instead of a necessity.

Now as this happened, there was an unintended consequence. People were not prepared to handle the number of ideas created by the explosion of innovation and growth. Rock Dwellers handled this idea congestion with two approaches: specialization and stratification.

Specialization

Because it is impossible for any one person to know all truth about all areas, Rock Dwellers developed specialties in different areas of knowledge. What makes the Rock Dweller comfortable with this strategy is the assumption we talked about before, the objective language. This allows for the specializations to grow independently, because with an objective language anyone can learn a specialization when and if it is needed. This is very helpful, as it has allowed knowledge to grow beyond one person's ability to know everything available. On the other hand, it has created systems of knowledge that are not integrated in their approach. "The result [of specialization] is a rapid increase in knowledge and also an inability to reduce all scientific knowledge to one comprehensive system."[12]

Stratification

As humanity continued to realize the amazing complexity of life and the world, people began to take a stratigraphic approach to knowledge. This idea is rooted in the desire for a "Grand Unified Theory" that would enable people to understand all knowledge.[13] The picture puzzle is an accurate representation of the Rock Dweller's desire for a system that works together without inconsistencies. The idea that there is something that encompasses everything and ties it together is critical to their thinking.

This desire layers the knowledge systems one on top of the other, with the most basic ones on the bottom. When problems are presented, Rock Dwellers go through the layers one by one, to explain the problem. First they describe the psychological reasons, then go to the social, then to the biological problems, and finally down to the atoms of physics. In the end, the problem can be explained by bits of matter acting in a certain way. "Ideas and feelings are reduced to chemical changes, and these to the movement of lifeless particles."[14] In this way, people have the ability to drive something down to the most basic elements. This allows positivism to understand a human at the most basic level by understanding the system that ties knowledge together.

Higher Math

There are some very attractive things about the positivist truth lens. It seems neat, controllable, and logical, but wearing this truth lens creates significant challenges. Let's first talk about the amount of math required. As we have already discussed, the influx of ideas is a very real challenge in today's world. In our modern world, Rock Dwellers must consider many more ideas on a daily basis than they ever had to before.

You have probably heard people say things such as, "I just can't keep up with it all!" or "I know I should be more familiar with that, but I have been too busy." Rock Dwellers require themselves to consider every idea and categorize it as either right or wrong, which leads them to respond in one of three basic ways:

1. They limit their interaction with new ideas to a volume they can process, and this leads them to spend more of their time in the subculture of people who share the puzzle they are putting together.

2. They force themselves to engage with many ideas, but make quick judgments and decisions about these ideas by peeling layers off with the goal of finding a root problem. They rely on other people's input heavily in order to keep up with the volume and the pace.

3. They allow much of the knowledge of the world to remain in specialty fields, knowing they can access those fields when and if they need to, putting off the discovery of a Grand Unifying Theory.

Because of a Rock Dweller's need to make a truth decision about every piece of knowledge, it may become easy to view the larger world as a constant threat. It is full of new information to be considered and processed. If life were relaxed and easy, processing new information might seem like fun. But most people's lives are characterized by stress, speed, and pressure, and because of this, Rock Dwellers are likely to look at new ideas and be overwhelmed. They might put off thinking about new things because of the work involved—just like people put off spending time on the elliptical machine.

An Issue of Control

This ability to achieve progress and define the hard facts of reality brings a great sense of control to the life of a Rock Dweller. By focusing on the *how*, life becomes a great game of cause and effect, with the ability to predict outcomes and shape the results. The world looks like "a perfect machine that could be controlled by those who had full knowledge of how it worked."[15]

The scientific method is one of the key tools that has developed to better discover new truth and control the processes that scientists observe. As a by-product, the scientific method has helped discipline and focus people in amazing ways, but essentially its main purpose is to control its subject matter by eliminating all subjectivity and making the search for knowledge objective. As subjective knowledge was eliminated from the search for truth in order to gain more control, the obvious impact was that people were viewed in this same sterile way—much like machines.

This sense of control spills over into all areas of life and guides how positivists deal with the natural world, their spiritual lives, and their relationships. Because this truth lens views all truth as knowable, all aspects of life are filtered through the rational mind before they are considered true. For a Rock Dweller, this need for control impacts areas such as scheduling a day, planning a career path, fixing the oil leak in a car, and on and on. This need for control is a natural result of positivism.

Building Silos

So if questions of *why* are not engaged in the natural world of positivism, then how do Christian Rock Dwellers deal with their spiritual realities and the natural world of science? The simple answer is that they build mental silos.

Think of a farm with silver silos standing neatly one next to the other. The adjacent fields are a patchwork of differently colored crops growing in the summer sun. As the crops are harvested the farmer keeps them separated and then stores them in different silos.

This farming image is another way to describe the stratigraphic approach to knowledge we talked about earlier. Because the discovery of the natural world is done through the scientific method and does not include matters of spirituality, Christians must build different silos for the different crops of knowledge in their lives. They put their spiritual discoveries in one silo and their natural discoveries in another. This solves the problem of trying to resolve the perceived differences between Christianity and the world of nature. "The only places spiritual realities impinge on the material world are in creation and in miracles that transcend or violate the laws of nature."[16]

Christianity and theology are left to develop on their own, using their own methods and language. It is interesting that with this freedom to develop an independent system of knowledge, the pursuit of spiritual knowledge mirrored the development of scientific research. So as positivism was beginning to provide a way to study the world, it influenced Christians as they studied the Bible so that "many came to see theology itself as a kind of science."[17]

But when people tried to integrate their spiritual knowledge with their natural knowledge, it was difficult to bridge the "chasm between religion and science."[18] Because of the inability to find harmony between religion and science, people began to use two different strategies. The one strategy is pictured above by the silos, where spiritual knowledge and natural knowledge are seen as dealing with different categories that do not overlap. Hiebert called this "compartmentalization."[19]

The other strategy is reductionism. When dealing with a problem, this strategy would lead those in the Christian realm to discount science and find a spiritual cause and solution. Meanwhile, the scientist would discount the spiritual and find a natural solution. "In the end, reductionism achieves integration between theology and science by denying the validity of one or the other of them."[20]

This results in the "secularization of everyday life" where people can live with their spiritual reality while still embracing science in their natural world.[21] As long as the positivist lives in the world of silos or reductionism, there is no conflict between the worlds of knowledge.

We think of a mom who wakes up in the night from the barking cough of a croupy child. For most moms the first thought will be to get out the Vicks and the humidifier to solve the problem. She doesn't panic because her pediatrician prepped her well for this experience. She understands the anatomy of the problem, knows when to call the doctor, and knows that the expected result will be a healthy child in three to five days. Because of the secularization of life, she does not feel any need to integrate her faith or spiritual belief into her midnight decision.

The next night, she has quite a different experience. That night when her son wakes again with croup, she immediately feels in her heart that she should pray. When her son's breathing begins to calm, she is amazed. She sees this as a miracle. God has intervened in the natural world. In this way, the positivist can live in both the spiritual and natural worlds without having to ask how they integrate.

This illustrates how Rock Dwellers can silo their experiences. The first night the mom was operating based on the knowledge in her scientific silo. The second night, she operated using the knowledge from her spiritual silo. Her truth lens did not change. She was simply moving from one knowledge system to another.

Faith through Knowing

Our assumption throughout this book is that faith is a gift from God that we cannot earn or measure. This is important to mention because this section will address the Rock Dwellers' passion for interpreting their faith through knowing. The challenge for many Christian positivists is that their way of knowing spills over into their Christian perspective on truth, the Bible, and faith.

Because the people took a scientific approach to their faith walk and study of the Bible, they began with the assumption that the Bible is completely knowable. So their main job in studying the Bible was to know more and more about it. Knowing became the main goal of their faith walk. And the questions they were trying to answer were those of the core truths or "the unchanging verities that underlie reality" of the Bible that could be applied in all circumstances. [22]

Rock Dwellers seek to know as much about their beliefs as possible. And because the Christian faith is based on knowing, there is a huge industry surrounding Bible studies and experts who say they know what our faith is supposed to look like. Since the knowing seems like such a big task, we often leave it to the specialists to figure out for us, as we leave biology to the biologists. In this way, our faith comes down to which system of knowledge about the Bible we align ourselves with. Some align with a certain denomination, others with a Bible teacher, or an organization. But in positivism, since only one theory can be correct, this is also applied to biblical truth. "Because each of us assumes that we are reading the biblical text honestly and without bias, we judge others as mistaken."[23]

One to One

Christians using the truth lens of positivism believe that if they honestly and without personal bias read the Bible, they can understand it completely. They believe that their understanding of the message can be an exact representation of what is in the Bible. Much like the picture puzzle we described, they begin putting pieces into their understanding of God's Word. "A positivist's stance on theology postulates a direct (sometimes referred to as one-to-one) correspondence between the Bible and theology—between the messages found in the text and the interpretation of them in the mind of the theologian, who is seen as an objective observer."[24] Unbiased information and credible sources are core values in the pursuit of understanding the Bible.

So if Rock Dwellers are discussing a Bible passage and have two different understandings of what the passage means, the positivist truth lens causes them to believe that one of them must be wrong. The objective is to figure out which one is in error and correct the problem. This conviction can be very good, bringing about study and work to understand the Bible better. This truth lens has also brought to the study of the Bible what Hiebert called "a high view of truth and absolutes."[25]

While this is its strength, the weakness is that it focuses on knowing about God instead of knowing God in relationship. This is a lesson we hear from our pastors and teachers on a regular basis, but many do not understand that the struggle with knowing God intimately has a lot to do with our truth lens. Another weakness is that being right is placed on a higher level than relationships. The arguments and divisions among us have much to do with our truth lenses. These discussions about theology keep us from dealing with practical issues, people's everyday problems, and how the Bible relates to those.

We hope you are beginning to understand life on the rocky side of the river. The Rock Dwellers live on their separate rocks because it helps them remain objective in their search. Their spirited debates stem from their need to find resolution and the one right way. Focusing on the *how* questions allows them to make great strides in their quality of life and progress. Their fear of the river comes from the assumption that if questioning one part of their structure of knowledge is allowed, some part of the system might not stand the scrutiny. In this case, the whole truth system must be abandoned.

It would be hard to say enough about the huge contribution the positivist truth lens has made to the history and development of our world. The contributions of the Rock Dwellers permeate all of modern life. However, we see that there are some drawbacks too. Some Rock Dwellers have seen these challenges and ventured into the river. Let's go down to the shore and explore the truth lens of the Island Dwellers and how it affects how they live, act, and interact with the people around them.

Chapter 4

INSTRUMENTALISM

The rocky side of the town was a nice place to live—with many amenities and comforts. This drew other people to settle on the rocky shore. As more people began to settle in and be part of the town, conflicts arose. Because the new people had different origins than the original settlers, they brought different ideas about how life should be lived. The community struggled to agree on issues that ranged from government to work ethics.

For many Rock Dwellers, the immediate response was to hold tightly to their way of looking at the world and resist these new ideas that contradicted what they knew to be true. But some of the Rock Dwellers were unable to dismiss the new ideas completely and were intrigued by what these new people were saying. The immigrants did not have the same understanding of the world or the same language that the original Rock Dwellers used. Arguments increased, and it became clear that they needed a solution to the growing diversity.

The new ideas caused people to group with others who saw things the same way. After a while the new group decided that it might be better to move somewhere else where they could live without conflict. To get some perspective, these seekers walked along the shore and thought together about what life might be like if people were allowed to look at truth differently. They wanted their perspectives to count. So as they looked around, they decided not to return to their community; instead they pushed on and settled on the small islands that populated the river.

Instrumentalism Summarized

The starting point of the instrumentalist truth lens comes from the question, How can we separate ourselves, including our experiences, culture, and perspective, from what we are learning? And if we can't, how can we know if we are being totally objective? Through this line of thinking the Island Dwellers realized that "there is no cold, totally objective reasoning."[1] They saw the claims of objectivity presented by the Rock Dwellers as illogical. They still assumed a real world, but because they couldn't see how they could possibly separate themselves and their personal perspectives from the knowledge they were gathering, they began to question all truth.

The Island Dwellers looked for a new way of thinking that allowed for subjective views of the world. They were searching for a truth lens that would value their personal experiences and perspectives. In order to understand their subjective knowledge, the instrumentalists looked outside themselves to the culture that was forming their experiences and assumptions. They knew that even the words they spoke and the understanding of those words came from the culture surrounding them.

Several key characteristics describe the Island Dwellers:

- They validate that there is a real external world to be explored and enjoyed, like the sandbars they live on.
- They see knowledge as real but subjective, defined by their own realities.
- They see truth as intensely personal because there are no bridges from island to island.
- They allow many theories and systems to exist at once and contradict each other without creating a crisis, because they value tolerance and personal belief above the need for larger agreement.

Cultural Creation

As people began to explore the depths of their own knowledge, they began to see knowledge as a cultural creation. You can think of this knowledge as a ham sandwich. When you read the two words *ham sandwich*, an image immediately pops into your mind. You can probably almost taste it. That image for Mindy is two soft pieces of Wonder Bread, a slice of Kraft cheese, and two pieces of deli meat—all wrapped in a brown paper bag to be opened at the ringing of the lunch bell. The image for Jon is a fresh baguette cut long-ways with ham slices stuffed in the middle of the loaf. The sandwich came from a small bakery in Caracas, Venezuela, and was eaten after a long bus ride.

We both think that we *know* what a ham sandwich is, but our ideas of the ham sandwich are very different. In this way, our knowledge is shaped by our cultures and experiences, with the language we use flowing from those. Both of us are content to have different meanings for the concept because we have no idea what the creator of the ham sandwich intended. He or she may have created something very different, like a panini from Italy or a hoagie from Philadelphia. The original design of the sandwich is not important to us personally. Therefore, we allow the word to mean something different for each of us based on individual culture and personal taste. And even if someone were to come forward with documentation of the exact intentions of the inventor of the ham sandwich, the instrumentalist truth lens would say that we cannot possibly receive that information in the way the originator intended because our culture and context is so different. One person could read the intent and end up making something like a Wonder Bread sandwich and another person might make something more like a panini.

So in the end, truth lenses rely heavily on the language we use. This is important because it will propel our communication that affects our relationships within the communities of River Town. Island Dwellers work to understand words within their present context. Hiebert explained it this way: "To understand words, we must understand the sentences and paragraphs in which they are found. To understand sentences and paragraphs, we must understand the social situations—the language games—in which they are spoken."[2] These language games are foundational to understanding meaning in the instrumentalist truth lens because culture creates the situations and scenarios that give the words meaning.

So it works a little like this: An idea is given to you within your community and culture. You bring that idea into your mind, and it immediately takes on a personal meaning that cannot be transferred to anyone else. So meaning starts in your community and dead ends in your mind—without a way to effectively transfer or share it. This way of accepting knowledge isolates you, making your understanding of the world completely personal.

But while you have isolated yourself in your individual knowledge, you have freed yourself to interact with whatever someone else tells you, whether it mirrors your knowledge or not. You can listen unthreatened to anything your neighbors want to tell you, and you can accept it, knowing that they also have personal understandings.

Hiebert described this: "If meaning is found in people's heads, then communication is measured not by the accurate transmission of objective facts, but by the inner images and feelings that are generated in the mind of the listener. Communication, therefore, must be receptor oriented. What is important is not what the sender means but what the listeners perceive."[3]

Island Dwellers talk very differently than the Rock Dwellers. When they speak, they are aware that the people they are talking to are filtering everything they say through their own personal experiences. Discussions don't center around finding truth, but on sharing experiences. "We use the same words, but we have the uneasy feeling that we are not all using them in the same ways."[4]

In the river, people build communities of belief on their small islands and enjoy sharing in a common idea of truth within the small community. However, they have no illusions that their truth is transferable to the next island. This inability to build bridges and gain true understanding is called incommensurability. Hiebert explained that this "means that ideas expressed in one language or culture cannot be accurately translated into other languages or cultures."[5] This is why the Island Dwellers are essentially isolated on their small islands with very few people who share their experiences and understanding.

One of the aspects that people love about the river environment is the richness of the language. There are millions of ways of looking at each idea, and you can mold and shape these many thoughts into inclusive prose and harmonious poetry. "Language, in other words, is not surface, precise and flat like mathematics. It is multivocal, rich and full of subtle nuances. This is what makes language so powerful, but this richness also makes it fuzzy and ambiguous."[6]

A great example of this richness of language is the song "Imagine" written by John Lennon. In it, he describes a world in which there's no heaven or hell, religion, countries, or possessions, and where everyone lives in peace. While we don't know the exact nature of Lennon's truth lens, the words of this song connect with how Island Dwellers see words and feelings as joined together. It also speaks to the very personal nature of knowledge in instrumentalism. Much about this truth lens is decided by intuition and feeling because reality does not go beyond a person's own perception of it.

But another thing we see in this song that is very evident in instrumentalism is community. One of the most encouraging things about this truth lens for many people is the dialogue that it allows with others who see the world very differently. Because truth is seen as very personal, you can build relationships with many people that you do not have very much in common with. By setting the ground rules of instrumentalism, each person is assumed to have his or her own truth, and this provides the freedom to build relationships. This is probably what Lennon was referring to when he referenced "sharing all the world."

But this general feeling of sharing is not true communication "because there is no neutral observation language and because there are no translation manuals for rival theoretical languages, [and] communication between people in different scientific paradigms is impossible. In fact, they cannot intelligently understand one another. They simply talk past each other. Rival theories become not merely different ways of looking at reality but different worlds and different realities."[7] Essentially, without a shared set of understandings, very little true communication takes place between people.

There is one way that people in the river find common ground. Simply put, an instrumentalist is happy to say that something is *true enough*. The importance of an idea rests in the ability to provide proof not of its truth but of its usefulness. This is also known as pragmatism. We use the word *pragmatic* to mean that if an idea works, it is true enough to solve my problem. Because instrumentalism sees the understanding of truth as resting in the individual, this value of pragmatism comes in handy when making decisions about what is true. Two people can agree that something is useful, and in this they can find common ground between them.

Hiebert called this idea a "useful fiction."[8] This does not mean that the Island Dwellers will purposefully take a false idea and use it anyway. It means that they do not believe that any fact or idea can be objectively labeled as true or false. Usefulness is the best criteria to decide whether or not to adopt an idea. We use this concept with children many times, to help them understand something we cannot fully explain. We say to the child at dusk, "The sun is going to sleep. Say goodnight to the sun." To the instrumentalist, this is not a lie or an assault on truth, it is a useful fiction that helps the child understand that they will not see the sun for a while, but that it will shine again tomorrow morning when "the sun wakes up."

Many Island Dwellers live in this world of pragmatism, not concerning themselves with proving things true or false, but focusing on solving problems. Hiebert explained, "If we cannot test for truth, on what basis can we judge between scientific theories? The answer is pragmatism—the 'useful fictions' that are good if they are useful and if they work. The purpose of science, therefore, is not to find truth about the external world but to control it for our own purposes."[9]

We see the results of pragmatism throughout our culture. With the value of progress well established in our culture, coupled with this unconcern about the truthfulness of ideas, the instrumentalist is forced to use pragmatism to continue to produce results.

In many cases you won't know what truth lens people are wearing by looking at their actions because of pragmatism. After study and argument has shown it to be sound, a Rock Dweller businessperson may believe in the proven truth of a particular marketing strategy. An Island Dweller may also use the same marketing strategy, not because it is proven to be true but because it works. The action is the same, but the truth lens is different. One businessperson acts from the objective and logical *proven* truth of something, while the other acts from its *usefulness*.

If a Rock Dweller can be thought of as working on a puzzle, filling in the details piece by piece, the Island Dweller can be thought of as creating a collage. Each addition represents an individual's experience in the world as seen through the culture. Every person adds a portion to the whole without being questioned about its validity. In this way, community interaction is about sharing and creating a beautiful expression of human experience. In the end, they view their lives as building a collage and sharing with the world all their ideas and experiences.[10]

If positivism approaches truth as constructing a large building, Island Dwellers are building one-room structures. New ideas are not threatening because they are not worried about a collapsing foundation. Instead, if an idea needs to be thrown out, they simply build a new structure. If an idea is useful, it is adopted. If in time it becomes useless, it is set aside.

Community Focused

Because of the importance of language to the Island Dwellers, truth begins in the community. We learn our language through the people around us and internalize it based on our experiences. The experiences with a community infuse meaning into the words. These words are the building blocks for a world of knowledge in the mind.

As the people settled on the sandy islands, they built communities based on common thoughts and experiences. Out of these similarities came the common vocabulary they used to build their individual understandings of the world.

Within this individualized perspective, how does community really work? As we discussed above, it seems as if community would be easier to attain with instrumentalism. After all, if you take away all the sticky issues of life, shouldn't we all get along splendidly?

But this did not happen. While the Island Dwellers found peace and unity at first, they began to move farther and farther apart in their thinking because the ideas they were accepting were so individualized. Their pragmatism allowed them to accomplish day-to-day tasks, but their truth lens did not provide a way to make connections. They could talk to one another about their worlds through a common vocabulary, but they had no assurance that the other person could understand, because they had internalized the words so differently.

Island Dwellers lived in community, but under the surface they were being driven apart as their personal realities matured. So as they developed more personal views of truth, they had less and less in common with their neighbors until they had nothing in common at all. "Each community, and ultimately each person, is imprisoned inside its own subjective worlds. The result is egocentrism and narcissism."[11]

Living Side by Side

Since the Island Dwellers are not able to prove anything right or wrong and believe they are unable to share their internal worlds of knowledge, this influences how they relate to each other. To see this in action, let's look at an example of a short-term missions trip the way our parents' generation may have approached it versus the way our own peer group may approach it.

A generation or two ago, a person going on a trip most likely viewed it through the truth lens of positivism and saw it as an opportunity to spread the gospel along with the benefits of modern Western society, assuming without question this would be beneficial. But with the truth lens of instrumentalism on the rise, a person going on a short-term trip today would likely choose to focus on humanitarian needs because it is hard for them to see how they could share Christ in such a different cultural context from their own. "Day-to-day encounters with other kinds of people raise the question of 'otherness.' How can people of different cultures and religions live together? The modern answer is that all people are free, within very wide limits, to seek their own home and to adopt and hold their own views, within the private sphere of life, of what is good and desirable."[12]

Back in River Town, the real test came for the Island Dwellers when one night the spring floods appeared suddenly and the sandbars shifted. Many islands grouped into one larger sandbar, and several groups of people found themselves living together. This challenged their truth lens. They wondered whether they could live together with people who viewed the world differently from them—views based on different paradigms and cultural creations.

This picture describes pluralism in our own world. The idea of pluralism simply means that many ideas and points of view can exist together without the need to find agreement. We see this everywhere. Hiebert observed, "The result has been a growing awareness of cultural and religious pluralism. No longer are people limited to certain territories. They are now found in great diversity in every city around the world."[13]

In the past, cultural and religious diversity was experienced when one person went to another place—like the early settlers or missionaries heading out from Europe. The initial response was to try to make the people they were visiting more like them to build a harmonious and unified community. Over time people began to see that there was value in other cultures. They approached a new culture from a position of understanding and dialogue without trying to change it. This change in thought process among anthropologists birthed the tools of instrumentalism that help people live with the growing awareness of pluralism. As the global economy exploded, people began to move about freely and settle in places where their views were not held by the general population around them.

Living side by side with very different people causes very different reactions. Throughout the past century as this movement of people progressed, we have seen violence, segregation, and the creation of enclaves. Instrumentalism came into this picture with practical tools to deal with the problem. It provided the ability to have differing views side by side without the need to harmonize them. Hiebert described it this way, "The postmodern answer to this growing pluralism is that different kinds of people must learn to live together; each community lives within its own enclave preserving its own distinctive, and each must tolerate the differences of the others."[14]

This truth lens became very useful in a pluralistic society, because it encourages people to allow others to live their lives their own way. This is not seen as weakness but strength. After all, for Island Dwellers living with your neighbor next door requires being able to accept a different view of truth. This concept can be viewed on a larger scale of a neighborhood or town. If an Island Dweller wasn't able to accept an environment of differing views, he or she would have to live on an island alone. For Island Dwellers, living in community necessitates tolerance. But even though they have been able to find a way to get along with other people, this pluralism also results in "doubt about the nature of themselves and the universe in which they live."[15]

Within the larger understanding of this truth lens and the reality of pluralism, there are some very well-known movements of thought. They are also very controversial. These movements have been labeled and discussed until they are almost stripped of any meaning. C. S. Lewis, in his book *Studies in Words*, described the destruction of words this way, "Verbicide, the murder of a word, happens in many ways. Inflation is one of the commonest; those who taught us to say awfully for 'very', tremendous for 'great', sadism for 'cruelty' and unthinkable for 'undesirable' were verbicides . . . But the greatest cause of verbicide is the fact that most people are obviously far more anxious to express their approval and disapproval of things than to describe them."[16]

Two words that have been treated this way are *postmodernism* and *relativism*. The concept of postmodernism cannot be separated from instrumentalism (and, for our purposes, with Island Dwellers). To be postmodern is to react to the positivism of modernity and science (personified through our Rock Dwellers) and to search for another way of interacting with the world. "Postmodernity focuses on the self and the now—on the concrete in the form of daily life as an alternative to theory."[17] This reaction to modernity leads to a lack of interest in history and a turning away from logic toward intuition and creativity. At the same time, "the cardinal postmodern sins are ethnocentrism and attempts to convert others to one's own beliefs and practices, or to control them."[18] This cultural and philosophical movement toward intuition and creativity is based on the instrumentalist truth lens, but it is not itself instrumentalism. Instrumentalism is the truth lens that helps individual people make decisions, but when many people hold the same truth lens the natural result is a movement—like postmodernity.

The other much-described movement is relativism. Many times when Hiebert talked about the river in our story, he referred to Peter Berger's analogy as the "stream of relativism."[19] The constant current of the water continues to pull the Island Dwellers downstream toward a relativist outlook. This doesn't always happen immediately, but it is a strong force in their lives. If they were to begin floating down the river past the sandbars, they would bob and sway into a world of relativism that ends only in an extreme meaninglessness—nihilism. Hiebert described relativism as the force that denies any ability to know truth.[20]

It is important to restate that to have the instrumentalist truth lens does not mean you are a part of the postmodern movement or that you are a relativist or nihilist. However, it does mean that you will be influenced by these two major forces.

Impact on Faith

While at first glance instrumentalism seems like a stranger to the Christian faith, it is very much a part of it. Instrumentalism does not negate a faith—it simply makes it completely personal. So in this truth lens, the focus of faith shifts away from shared beliefs and moves to a posture of dialogue between many different understandings of faith and many different theologies. Hiebert described the task of an instrumentalist in evangelism as, "to join people in other religions in their search for dignity and freedom, and to learn from them what we find helpful for ourselves."[21]

If you hold this truth lens, you may have strong feelings about what your faith means to you, but you are unwilling to make the jump to say that others must also hold those feelings. You have no certainty that the knowledge that you use to make moral decisions will work for anyone else. In this reality, "Christianity becomes an intensely personal concern expressed in a closed community of faith."[22]

In positivism the focus of truth and faith is one to one, but in instrumentalism it changes to one plus one. Pluralism presents the Island Dweller with millions of potential views on the Bible. It is in this pluralism that they use the tool of dialogue to explore theologies. They are not looking for one theology. Instead, they are looking to understand what is useful from the many theologies to apply to their personal faith. "It is our human search for God—our God-talk, not God's revelation to us. This means that we must speak of 'theologies,' not Theology, for there are as many theologies as there are human points of view."[23]

Instrumentalism brings back the narrative of humanity into the process of understanding faith. It values subjective knowledge that is important to bringing back the warmth of our relationship with God. But as it does this, it also introduces some serious problems which take the form of relativism and produce the isolation of a completely personal faith walk.

A Driving Doubt

We hope you have a better understanding of the Island Dwellers as you watched them develop their communities of thought on the sandbars. The truth lens of instrumentalism prepared them for the storm that brought them together as the sandbars merged. They were able to live peacefully with many views, but a growing sense of doubt overshadowed their tolerance in the face of so many differences. Though the Island Dwellers escaped some of the problems of the rocky shore, they lived with the danger of the swift currents of relativism that eroded and shaped their sandbars. Doubt was the strong force that drew many of them into the currents.

Some of the Island Dwellers saw their friends being drawn into the current by doubt, and though they liked the ability to coexist with many other people and their viewpoints, they longed for security and true community that would relieve the intense isolation they felt. Some went back to the rocky shore and worked to fit into the culture they had once resisted. Others, not wanting to return to the rocky shore, looked past the sandbars to the valley on the far shore.

Chapter 5

CRITICAL REALISM

After one particularly scary storm in River Town, with sand-bars shifting all around them, several islanders decided it was time to make their move. They knew going back to the rocky shore would never give them the environment they were searching for, so they pressed on into the unknown to explore the far shore of the river.

The Far Shore

It took quite an effort to navigate the currents, the bogs, and shallow waters. But finally they emerged and were surprised at how solid the ground felt beneath their feet after their time on the sand. They began to hike further away from the shore. On the far shore, they found some beautiful valleys at the base of a mountain forest. They settled in one of these valleys, but before building they took time to plan their little settlement. They had learned many lessons from their time on the rocky shore and their time in the river. This settlement would have no mounds to separate people, as they experienced on the rocky shore; it would have many inter-connections that they lacked on the sandy islands; and it would be built on solid ground, which they believed to be knowable truth. As they talked and drew up plans, they each became more excited. Out of their discussions came a community of neat little homes connected by wide roads, parks, and courtyards. There was excitement in the air as they dreamed about what their life would be like.

Critical Realism Summarized

As we look at the Valley Dwellers' approach to truth, through which we'll explore critical realism, we will immediately see some significant differences from the approaches of the positivism of the Rock Dwellers and the instrumentalism of the Island Dwellers. However, it is also important to realize that critical realism builds on both positivism and instrumentalism and seeks to deal with some of the main challenges that we have already addressed. In essence, we can summarize critical realism with the phrase *the truth you know and the truth you are learning*. As we explore the many elements of critical realism, we will see how this phrase represents the essence of this truth lens.

You may have noticed that the three truth lenses we are discussing have assumed that a real world exists. This is a key point to be reemphasized. The truth lenses used in River Town do not include those that deny a knowable, real world that can be experienced. Each truth lens in our journey allows people to discover truth and provides a footing on which they can live their lives. This means that these truth lenses can provide a way to understand and apply the truth of the Bible. With that in mind, the analysis of each truth lens is not to differentiate which one can give us a way to live out our faith. Instead, we are asking the question, Which of these truth lenses encourages a humble understanding of the truth God reveals as we live out our faith more completely and fully?

One of the core assumptions of critical realism is that knowledge is more than factual information.[1] Instead of looking at knowledge as a picture puzzle to be put together or a collage of experiences, this truth lens takes a group of pictures and pulls them together into a greater image—a montage.

As we sat around the table at his home that summer, Dr. Hiebert pulled out slides to illustrate this concept. One slide showed, at first glance, a granulated picture of a face. But on closer inspection, we realized that this face was made up of many small faces—each separate and unique.[2]

In critical realism, personal experiences, ideas, feelings, facts, and pieces of information make up knowledge. But unlike the collage of images instrumentalism creates, the image revealed in the creation of a montage brings purpose to the whole. This leads a Valley Dweller to a broader understanding of truth. Discovering truth is not about separating people from objective data, but bringing them together into greater understanding. "Critical realism also restores emotions and moral judgments as essential parts of 'knowing' and argues that these do not necessarily negate the objectivity of scientific observations."[3]

Bridging Knowledge Gaps

There were two things that drove the inhabitants of River Town into the river and then onto the other shore. The first move came because there was no room for other views or perspectives, and the second move came because there was no solid foundation on which to relate. Positivists strove so hard toward objectivity that they denied personal experience. Instrumentalism solved this problem by putting knowledge completely in the mind. But this left Island Dwellers unable to share truth with their neighbors or add to truth through another's experiences. But on the far shore, people found a place where they could combine the strengths of both of these views. In so doing, they could have both the objective knowledge gained through study and the subjective knowledge of their experience. "Critical realist epistemology [truth lens] strikes a middle ground between positivism, with its emphasis on objective truth, and instrumentalism, with its stress on the subjective nature of human knowledge. . . . It affirms the presence of an objective truth but recognizes that this is subjectively apprehended."[4]

The first two truth lenses we looked at base the search for truth on logic. Island Dwellers moved away from the objective search for truth of the Rock Dwellers because they saw that they couldn't logically remove themselves from their perceptions. They reasoned that the only truth they could count on was in their own minds. They arrived at this conclusion through the same system of logic used by the settlers on the rocky shore.

But critical realism also allows for other ways of knowing. While Valley Dwellers value logic as one way of knowing, they see a world with many other ways to gain knowledge. One example is history; there are many things that we can learn through the perspective and process of history. This is a way of knowing that is not bound up in logic, but in narrative. The far shore of the river allows for history to sit at the table with logic and objective truth and help paint a fuller picture. Another example is knowledge of people. Unlike biology, which studies the functions of the human body, and unlike sociology, which studies the functions of how humans relate, when we have a relationship with someone and when we talk about knowing them, it goes beyond objective facts about the person to an understanding of the person as a human. "Critical realism . . . broadens the concept of rationality to include other types of reasoning. It recognizes the role of metaphors, analogies, and other tropes in shaping human thought."[5]

Approximate Knowledge

All of these aspects of critical realism allow Valley Dwellers to have a fuller understanding of their world. Another key tool in this effort is the ability to use approximate knowledge. "Knowledge is always partial and often flawed, . . . but we can gain a better understanding of truth. In this way knowledge can be seen as approximate and still useful."[6] An example of this is when the lights go out in the house. We don't need to check every light bulb in the house to know when the fuse has blown. Testing two or three lights in different parts of the house is probably enough to drive us to the fuse box to flip the switch. This makes critical realism actionable.

Not only do we know the objective truth that serves as a foundation, but we also understand the warmth, humanity, and connections of personal experience that allow us to draw the lines between the objective truth and our day-to-day living. This enables an understanding of truth that helps us to create a plan of action. Critical realism values both data as well as personal understanding of those facts. Because of this, it allows for the interaction between these ways of knowing. It enables us to make decisions based on the information we know in different ways. History and intuition would be two ways of knowing that are not based on logic.

This becomes valuable when we are trying to sort out a problem at work, home, or school. If a project is not going well, we look at the plan and how it is being implemented. But we also look to the people who are doing the work. How do they feel about the project? Are there conflicts between people that are slowing down the process? By coupling our objective knowledge and data about the project with our personal perceptions and understanding of the people involved, we are better able to make decisions on how to get the project back on track.

Language

This warmth of human perception flows into the idea of words. For Valley Dwellers, words do not have the one-to-one correlation that they do on the rocky shore. Words also do not solely live in the mind, as on the sandy islands. Instead, this relationship creates a triangle of interaction—a concept introduced by Charles Pierce—where the word in ink refers to the object and also creates images in our minds of feelings and memories connected to that word. This interaction helps us build meaning and gives us a fuller understanding of the word. This is helpful as we strive to learn more about our world and about each other.[7]

This view of language allows us to know things in different ways. We think of the crime dramas on television where a common plot finds the characters looking at all the evidence they have gathered from the scene. They study the bits of information, searching their minds for a theory that would tie the evidence together, when suddenly a word or photo or smell evokes personal images that guides them in further investigation. Personal experiences with the data are tied not only to the crime scene but also to past personal experiences. All these perceptions are useful when trying to arrive at a solution.

Getting Out of the Silos

The Valley Dwellers found a way to get out of the mental silos created on the rocky shore. When positivism created the tool of silos, it became very difficult to make informed decisions that factor in different knowledge systems. For example, when trying to make a decision about your health, critical realism allows you to integrate your faith and your interactions with a medical professional. It also allows you and your healthcare professional to integrate factors like chiropractic care, nutrition, and so on. In positivism one of these knowledge systems would rule out the others. You could move from one silo to the other, but you would have to reject the one you had come from. Critical realism says that you can use information from many knowledge systems to better understand your situation. It also says that if you and others share a worldview, then you can interact from these different knowledge systems with some confidence in understanding each other. So to use our medical example, if your doctor, your chiropractor, and you have a common worldview that defines how you look at the world, then you can translate among your realities and learn together.

Sharing Discoveries

Let's leave River Town for a minute and imagine that we are in a jungle. The sounds of the jungle are everywhere. Exotic birds call out to the wild in search for their mates. Insects create an ever-present buzz that sets the mood. And once in a while we hear the rustle of some large mammal stalking through the underbrush searching for lunch. Beyond the noises of the animals, the heat is another constant force. It pushes down like a French press making coffee. The oppressive heat influences every decision of those who live under its reign.

On a day like most others, we witness three blind men walking together on one of the many paths that crisscross the jungle. They have been friends for many years. Theirs is a friendship born of common life experiences and of necessity. Their blindness binds them together, but beyond that they need each other for support and protection.

So on this particular day, these men are making their way slowly along the path to one of their favorite bathing areas. Since it is a long trek into the jungle, the whole exercise makes a full-day activity.

As they progress tentatively down the path, something stops them suddenly. Like dominoes, the first one hits the obstacle, and then the other two run into him. This object had never been on this path before. Immediately, the little band is fearful of what might be in front of them. They know too well that the jungle is full of danger, and they quickly work together to find out what is in front of them.

The first blind man moves to the left and feels a long, straight object. It extends upward as far as he can reach and has a rough surface. He deduces that this obstacle must be a tree. The second blind man explores the part of the object directly in the path. He gropes around to find four stout objects holding up a larger surface. He remembers the stages erected by the villagers for festivals and assumes that this must be some sort of stage. The third blind man walks to the right and is able to touch a rope-like object swinging vigorously back and forth. As he grabs hold of it, he feels its frayed edges and concludes that this must be a rope structure of some kind.

As the men explore the obstacle, they shout out to each other what they have discovered. But the discrepancies become obvious and an argument ensues. The frustration is that they cannot prove their positions because they cannot see the object. So they give up, inch their way around it, and grumpily proceed on toward their bathing spot.

You may recognize this story as it is an old one. If you haven't heard it, the end of the story is rather comical. These three men all experienced different parts of the object in their path. The tree, the stage, and the rope were actually all parts of one reality—namely the trunk, body, and tail of an elephant. But these three men could not come to that conclusion because they were making their conclusion about reality based solely on what they personally experienced. Now imagine how that story might have been different if the three men had pooled their knowledge and made a group analysis. No doubt, they would have come to a different conclusion that was closer to the truth than where their individual conclusions led them.

Remember that these men were from the same culture and background, so they probably shared a worldview. So if they had been Valley Dwellers, they could have potentially come to the conclusion that they were all touching a very large mammal. They may not, at first, have come to the conclusion that it was an elephant, but their pooled knowledge would have still been very useful.

As Hiebert explained, "If these men shared their findings with one another and realized that each felt a part of the whole, they could come closer to the truth."[8] Instead of the one man thinking that the elephant was a tree, he would have an expanded understanding. And if the men kept discovering together, they would learn more about their subject and come closer to the full truth about the object in front of them. Their personal experiences would be affirmed, their biases would be held in check, and they would all come away with a clearer understanding of the elephant. This describes how different knowledge systems can share information and build a fuller understanding of the truth.

Information can be translated between knowledge systems.[9] This is possible because, while we may be looking at something from a different perspective than another person, we still inhabit the same physical world and our minds are designed in similar ways. This creates a commonality that allows us to bridge the gaps. Another important point is that if two people are looking at the world from different knowledge systems (like our doctor and chiropractor) but share the same worldview, then they can translate information through what Hiebert called a "Metacultural Translation Grid." This can be thought of as both people stepping outside of their knowledge systems and studying each one together. Through communicating in this way, they can translate and talk to each other.

This may be thought of as communication between different but compatible software programs. If your word processing and spreadsheet programs were created by the same company for the same operating system, then sharing information between them can be seamless. This is like when two people from different fields of knowledge share a worldview and truth lens and decide to talk with one another about their discoveries. Sometimes there is some adjustment and work involved to get the two to really understand each other, but it's possible. More difficult problems arise when you try to take information from two software programs that are not compatible. Most of us have seen the garbled text that results. We experience the same type of frustration when we try to understand someone with a different worldview and truth lens.

Another tool that critical realism provides is the ability to act on partial knowledge. We can look at the information in front of us and make an informed decision while understanding that we still have more to learn about the situation. Hiebert used the example of a pixelated image. We don't have to have the newest digital camera with the most megapixels in order to know that the image in front of us is our grandmother on her seventieth birthday. A low-quality cell phone photo does the job just as well, even though it captures much less detail and exactness. Our minds have a great ability to fill in what is missing. This is core to a critical realist view of knowledge. By focusing on the relationships among the bits of knowledge we learn, we are freed from having to dig out every last detail in order to take action. Critical realism allows us to see knowledge as maps of reality. Just as a map does not represent every detail of life, our knowledge doesn't have to be complete to be useful.[10]

Hiebert addressed our inability to know truth fully when he wrote, "Reality is too complex for our finite minds to grasp in total. We need complementary models to comprehend it."[11]

Useful Maps

Hiebert talked a lot about maps to describe human knowledge. As we've said, a map is not an exact representation of reality, but it is an actionable representation. This illustrates that human knowledge and the world are not in one-to-one correspondence. When you pull that map out of the glove compartment of your car or print out an Internet map showing you how you get from your house to the doctor's office, you do not see everything that is really there. Those maps don't show you what the fence looks like on the house two doors down, but they do give you enough information to guide you to your appointment. Hiebert said it this way, "Meaning in maps is not the sum of bits of information and truth. It is the configuration that orders bits of information into an interpretive whole."[12]

Because a Valley Dweller can accept a map as a valid tool for understanding the world, the entire truth does not have to be known for that person to live, grow, interact with others, and make decisions. In fact, the map allows you to understand the basics that are known while learning about the other pieces of information that are not yet known. This truth lens accepts that there is truth we know and can agree on and also there is truth we are learning and must discover together.

That is the key to this truth lens. It is important to stress that critical realism affirms knowledge and truth as concrete and knowable. But instead of believing that the whole truth is knowable and understandable, it leaves a place for mystery. And beyond mystery, this truth lens says that knowing isn't solely about understanding facts—you have to understand the context of those facts in order to understand their meaning.

Culture and Community

Positivism and modernity are connected just as instrumentalism and postmodernity are linked. So what is the next movement? Hiebert described the cultural movement associated with critical realism as globalism. This great cultural movement is embodied by the global economy that drives us. But more importantly, as the world has become connected and engaged as a single entity, the issues that we must face have been joined. Think about issues such as the environment, terrorism, identity theft, and the global strength of the economy. These are issues that impact everyone on the planet in one way or another. "All the crucial problems have become world problems, and nothing essential can happen anywhere that does not concern us all."[13]

Into this brave world of oneness we are thrust, and with this new world comes unique challenges. We must find ways to understand the cultures and peoples around us and engage them in solving these significant problems. In this reality, critical realism provides a way forward.

A Process of Learning

As we laid the foundation for critical realism, we talked about *the truth you know and the truth you are learning*. Learning in community helps in this process. Much of the knowledge of the world lies in the understanding of others. By working together and through humble interaction, we can better understand each other and gain a richer understanding of any topic.

During this process of learning, we bring our personal biases and perspectives to the table. When we learn in community, these biases are revealed through collaboration and discussion. Hiebert referenced I. C. Jarvie when he said that the process becomes a "powerful corrective against the subjective biases of individual scholars."[14]

There are two parts to this process. The first part is setting the stage by defining what you will be thinking about, what words you'll be using, what standards, and so on. Hiebert called these "preunderstandings."[15] The second part is taking what you have learned and checking it through group interaction with the goal of gaining a better understanding of truth.

The implications of this in our lives are pretty significant. It means that while there is a baseline of truth that humankind has been able to understand and apply practically, the whole picture is much greater. There is room for new ideas, new interpretations, and new discoveries. This truth lens allows us to not be threatened by new ideas that seem to contradict the truth that we believe in.

Instead of rocking our faith, we understand that there is truth we are learning. In that context we are able to take this new piece of information and hold it up to what we already know. This does not mean that we simply accept contradicting views, but that we can work through these views as a process of developing a better understanding. In the context of theology, Hiebert stated that we must "deal with these differences . . . where contradictions do emerge, they must be resolved by further examining the Scriptures."[16]

One example of this is environmentalism. Creatures of modernity have a certain relationship with the environment—we have dominated it and used it to create our quality of life. We know what the Bible says about the environment based on God's commands to Adam. So we try to rule over the world and, at the same time, keep it from being destroyed or badly damaged.

But what if an African Christian of premodern thought came to your church and gave a talk on the environment? His different relationship with the earth would probably have given him different insights into Genesis 1. His insights might be new information that could broaden your understanding of the truth. In this way, you can learn from others who have the same framework, but have vastly different experiences and feelings.

You see how the basic truth from the Bible about God's commands to Adam and Eve did not change. You as a person born of modernity and your African friend of pre-modern thought have read the same words from this Bible passage, but you may have different perspectives about it. Sharing those with each other allows both of your understandings to grow without threatening either of your beliefs.

One example stands out to us. There have been many Sunday school classes that we have participated in and loved over the years. In one of our classes, we had two great teachers: one was a lawyer from a large technology company and the other was a pastor. Both were U.S. citizens and part of middle-class America. Each had his own style of teaching, but both brought a very familiar message to us.

Then one Sunday we had a guest speaker. He was an African serving as a missionary in another African country. The lesson he taught from the Bible was so different from anything we had heard before. The way he looked at the Bible passage was completely new to us. To this day we remember him.

Many of you reading this book will probably have a similar story. You have had the experience of seeing a familiar passage through someone else's eyes, and this brought it to life in an entirely new way. This is what we mean by the truth we know and the truth we are learning. The critical realist truth lens establishes a firm foundation of what we know, but then relishes in the drama and mystery of what we still have to learn.

How will we live differently when we put on the truth lens of critical realism? First, a sense of humility begins to overshadow our interactions with the world. This may come in an instant or grow over time, but the assumption that we are on a journey to discover truth will color our experience. Through the practice of thinking about what we think with, we can approach other cultures in a posture of learning and move closer to the biblical worldview for which we are striving.

Valley Dwellers with the truth lens of globalism assume that they can share the knowledge of the world with each other and therefore can learn more truth together. Because community is important to learning, collaborative learning becomes a habit for those wearing the critical realist truth lens. This results in cooperation becoming more important than competition. Winning is no longer the trophy of truth, but truth itself becomes the prize we can all share.

Faith Implications

It is important for Christians to consider how understanding the Bible looks through the critical realist truth lens. Hiebert affirmed that the discovery of truth for a critical realist must start with the Bible, but he went on to say that it is realized in community, "Finally, theologizing must be done in community. It is ultimately the task not of individuals but of the church."[17]

This has not always been the case. On the rocky shore, understanding the Bible was seen as something that could be an exact representation of the Bible. The Bible itself and an understanding of it were seen as interchangeable. On the islands, a million understandings of the Bible could be accepted because knowledge of the mind could not be transferred or affirmed. On the far shore, the Bible is seen as having the final authority, but Valley Dwellers believe that looking at the Bible in light of the context of culture and personal perspectives is the key to discovering its truth.

Valley Dwellers strive to approach the Bible with humility, knowing that they can affirm facts as true, but knowledge is finite and partial. "We may 'see through a glass darkly,' not because of the limits of divine revelation, but because of the limits of our human knowledge."[18] Because of this, there is hope for continued understanding, and room for the Holy Spirit's teach-ing. "Furthermore, we must remember that God is continually at work in his church, shaping and reshaping it into his likeness."[19]

By creating what Hiebert called "hermeneutical communi-ties,"[20] the Valley Dweller's search for understanding truth takes on a whole new dimension. First of all, truth becomes something larger than any one subgroup, culture, or people group. If we are learning in community, then there are opportunities for each member to bring new perspectives and a richer understanding to any subject. Secondly, we avoid the pitfalls of a truth lens that is completely individualistic. In community, one person cannot claim complete understanding and reject the ideas of others. Finally, learning in community fits with the fact that God is work-ing in his church around the world through history, giving new insights and understandings as his people seek to know him.

An example of this is the churches of the Global South. After the significant church growth movements of the nineteenth and twentieth centuries, the church in the Global South (the southern hemisphere where Christianity is growing the fastest) is developing and coming into its own. As it does this, it is interpreting the Bible through its own cultures and experiences and beginning to write and share these ideas with the world. These ideas are also spreading as the Global South begins to send missionaries out to other parts of the world—including the increasingly post-Christian West.

As this happens, the African church, the Asian church, and the Latin American church are looking at the same Bible, but are asking different questions. Because of this and very different truth lenses, their understandings may look and sound different, but the truth of the Bible is the same. Hiebert explained, "Theologizing must be led by the Holy Spirit, who instructs us in the truth. We need also to work in the lives of believers in other contexts. Theologizing must also affirm the priesthood of all believers and recognizes that they must and will take the universal message of the Bible and apply it to their own lives and settings."[21]

Conclusion

Critical realism is a balance between instrumentalism and positivism. It takes the belief that truth can be known and shared from positivism and balances it with the individuality of our perceptions that we find in instrumentalism. It tempers the certainty with tolerance, coming away with a humble approach to knowledge and learning. When we swim across the river, we find our pride washing away along with the isolation of both positivism and instrumentalism and being replaced with humility and community. Our despair changes to hope as our journey of learning together continues on the far shore of the river.

At first, the Rock Dwellers were concerned about watching their neighbors going into the river. Seeing some swept away into the threatening hopelessness was hard. Many of them made it a point to stand on the shore and call their neighbors back, but they didn't offer any answers for the nagging questions that sent them into the water in the first place. They worried, wondering if there was any hope for them because they could not see the far shore of the river.

Then one day the Rock Dwellers met some Valley Dwellers who had come back to describe the beautiful community they had built on the far shore. At first, the Valley Dwellers sounded strange. Their language wasn't quite like before, and they didn't engage in debate as they used to. They were no longer using the language of the Rock Dwellers. Instead, their approach was engaging, inviting, and non-confrontational. They invited a journey for the whole person, not just the mind. Some Rock Dwellers were excited, but a little scared. They knew that to get to the far shore, they had to get into the water and go through the river.

Chapter 6

EXPERIENCING TRUTH IN LOVE

R oberto felt his responsibilities lift as the traffic-induced smog dissipated. Leaving San José on a Friday afternoon was never easy. Everyone in Costa Rica appeared to have the same thought: Let's go to the beach! That was where Roberto was headed, and with some open highway ahead, he didn't care how many urbanites might be tailing him.

As the dense jungles raced past, Roberto's busy life as a hospital administrator blurred, and he focused on the reason for his trip. That reason was sitting next to him in shorts and a tattered concert t-shirt. For a second, Roberto tried to remember which of his son's favorite bands the old shirt represented, but then shook his head and tried to concentrate on navigating through the traffic.

His son Carlos had been begging him for weeks to go sailing. Yes, sailing . . . *How did I ever become a sailor?* Roberto asked himself as he scanned the horizon for a gas station. It sure hadn't been intentional. A doctor at the hospital had been going through a midlife crisis and all of a sudden decided that an airplane fit his style more than the little sailboat he already had. One thing led to another, and Roberto became the owner of a slightly used, much discounted, little sailboat.

"So how fast do you think it will go, Dad?" asked Carlos. Roberto answered with a grin, "Maybe the better question is, How fast should we go? Remember our last lesson, don't you?" Carlos and Roberto both grimaced, remembering when Roberto was thrown overboard when an unexpected swell caused the boat to pitch wildly.

Ever since the boat had entered Roberto's life, his son had been fascinated. If it hadn't been for Carlos, they would have never taken lessons or invested in a place to dock the boat at the closest marina in Puntarenas. Now that the lessons were over, it was time for their first solo trip. Roberto had been anxious about it all week, but as San José faded into the horizon, his anxiety decreased and his excitement rose.

When they pulled up to the marina, Carlos bounded from their old SUV with all the pent up energy of a teenager. Roberto, who was getting more nervous by the minute, inhaled deeply and then stepped out of the car onto the sandy parking lot pavement.

As Roberto stood at the stern of the boat looking out at the sea, his son buzzed around him, preparing the rigging and loading supplies and bringing the sails topside. Roberto shook his head and tried to relax. After all, he knew what he was doing. Months of lessons and practice should make this easy, but this was, after all, the first time out alone.

Carlos had already climbed into the cockpit and was ready to go. The plan was to sail down the coast for a few hours, sleep on board, and then fish the next day. It sounded simple enough, Roberto thought as he made his way to the cockpit to get underway.

To Roberto's relief, things went smoothly. The waves sprayed the two novice sailors as they hit the bow, and the two took turns manning the helm and trimming the sails. As Roberto walked along the windward side of the boat, he still felt a bit uneasy without land underneath his feet. He looked longingly out at the emerald jungle floating by. Part of him wished he could be lying on the beach with a hotel room waiting for him that evening, rather than swaying on the same boat where he would sleep that night.

Finally, they arrived at the spot where they would anchor. Roberto readied the ground tackle on the deck so he could set the anchor well. When everything was prepared, he and Carlos let down the anchor; following each step as if the instructor was still sitting beside them.

Roberto was amazed at Carlos' energy and excitement. This teenager who could hardly get out of bed before noon was working hard and loving it. Roberto, on the other hand, was ready for bed. After a light supper, they settled into the very cramped quarters below.

In the middle of the night, Roberto woke up suddenly. He sensed the ship was moving. He wondered whether the boat was simply swinging on its anchor or if something was amiss. How was he supposed to know what it felt like when this was his first time? He went up on deck, found a flashlight, and took a look. *Was the shore that close last night?* he wondered.

Suddenly, he heard a scraping sound as the boat lurched starboard. Roberto almost lost his balance, but managed to stay standing. He immediately went to the bow and checked his anchor. *That's the problem!* he realized. The anchor was dragging. Somehow it had broken loose from the seabed.

Sweat beads formed on his brow as his mind raced. He remembered his sailing classes and tried desperately to remember the next steps to take at a moment like this. Roberto spent the next two hours by himself raising the anchor and trying to fasten it to the bottom. Each time it came loose, the boat drifted closer to the shore. It was hard to see how close they were in the dark, but Roberto knew that if he didn't do something soon they would be hard aground.

Exhausted, he slumped onto the deck, holding the ground tackle as his tears surfaced. A long week of worries and stress overcame him, and his mind shifted to the present. *Why didn't Carlos get up?* he wondered. Then it hit him like a wave crashing over his boat—Carlos was trusting in his dad to keep him safe, but Roberto's own trust was in this little anchor. The comparison jarred him like a boat suddenly running aground. Was there something bigger that deserved his trust?

We're all searching for those things we can trust and believe in. But just as Roberto wanted to trust his anchor, many times we choose to trust in things to hold us steady that are only a part of the whole. Finding truth we can trust is a lot like Roberto's adventure in anchoring his boat. It is not simply letting down a piece of iron and calling it a night. It is an intricate balance of interdependent factors resulting in a well-secured vessel. Anchoring a boat takes practice and experience. It takes putting knowledge to practical use in the spray and wind and weather of a hundred days at sea. Experiencing truth is like that. We can read books all day, take lessons, and even go out to sea; but until we've practiced truth and seen it in different circumstances, we only have a partial understanding.

Roberto and Carlos did not run aground that night. Roberto realized that in setting the anchor the night before, he had misjudged the amount of chain he needed on the bottom to help the anchor hold. In his inexperience, he underestimated the depth of the water, and through his struggle, he realized how hard it is to get security in the water. That night was a watershed moment in his life as a sailor.

Faith, Hope, and Love

Through this experience Roberto painfully learned how much he did not know. He experienced just a taste of the breadth of knowledge necessary to be a skilled sailor. It wasn't enough to know the basic theoretical concepts of sailing—Roberto had to use them under different conditions to gain a deeper understanding of how to sail. This is an example of the truth we know and the truth we are learning. We build on the knowledge we have by using it and being open to more understanding. We don't simply put truth in a pocket and call it a day; we continue to learn more about the truth we know by living it out in our daily experiences. The truth does not change, but our understanding and our experience applying truth changes dramatically.

Many times we relegate our experience of truth to the realm of belief. But what if there is more to truth than the act of believing?

We would like to propose that there is a holistic way to experience truth that goes beyond belief to include two other key dimensions. This holistic experience of truth is found in 1 Corinthians 13, famously known as the love chapter because it has some of the most powerful language in the Bible about the importance of love.

Our interest in this chapter comes out of the tension between two characteristics of God: truth and love. For Christians, there is a temptation to walk in either the love of God or the truth of God without walking in both at the same time. Either we want to save a relationship by looking away from the truth of God or we believe we should uphold the truth of God even at the expense of a relationship. In our desire to love people, we may feel helpless to hold tightly to truth, and in our desire to see truth upheld in an immoral world, we may become paralyzed in loving people. Knowing that God is described as both love and truth, we can turn to 1 Corinthians 13 for clarity. How do God's truth *and* his love relate?

Here the apostle Paul was challenging believers in Corinth to think about their motivations. The church was embroiled in controversy, sin, and confusion, and he challenged their thinking by focusing them on one of the most basic motivations of their faith: love.

This should not surprise us. The Ten Commandments given to Moses are all about loving God and loving others. Jesus prefaced his mission in John 3:16 by saying, "For God so loved the world." Jesus went on in John 15 to define his relationship with us and subsequently our relationship with God in terms of *abiding* in his love. In verses 9 and 10 of that chapter Jesus said, "As the Father has loved me, so have I loved you. Now remain in my love. If you obey my commands, you will remain in my love, just as I have obeyed my Father's commands and remain in his love."

The beauty of Paul's words in 1 Corinthians 13 is that he was inspired to define why love is so important. In the first part of the chapter, he set the stage by tackling motive. He listed all of the activities that the church in Corinth valued and that we value today: tongues, prophecy, understanding, faith, generosity, and bravery. He said that without love these are worthless to God. In doing this, he asked the Corinthians to examine what was motivating their good works. If they were obedient to God's commands but did not serve in love, God did not value their service.

Then in verses 4-6 Paul provided us with a beautiful definition of love that is both inspiring and daunting. But then Paul wrote something very strange. Verses 8-12 present three examples, one right after another. After he described love with such clarity, he then gave these examples that may throw the reader into a state of questioning.

Love's Journey of Learning

The first example is in verses 8-10: "Love never fails. But where there are prophecies, they will cease; where there are tongues, they will be stilled; where there is knowledge, it will pass away. For we know in part and we prophesy in part, but when perfection comes, the imperfect disappears." In this picture Paul explained that love is an eternal quality and preferable to any earthly gift such as prophecy, tongues, or knowledge. Our earthly understandings and spiritual abilities are far from perfect. The Matthew Henry Commentary describes it this way, "Our best knowledge and our greatest abilities are at present like our condition, narrow and temporary."[1]

Love's Journey of Growth

The second example is in verse 11: "When I was a child, I talked like a child, I thought like a child, I reasoned like a child. When I became a man, I put childish ways behind me." In this word picture, Paul taught that our understanding of love grows and develops. He gave us a glimpse into how God works with us by talking about how we have developed as people. Anyone who has been around children knows what it is like to try to explain something in a simple way so a child will understand. As children grow, explanations and discussions become deeper and more involved. Their worlds expand, and they are able to grasp greater pieces of the big picture.

Love's Journey of Relationship

The third example is in verse 12: "Now we see but a poor reflection as in a mirror; then we shall see face to face. Now I know in part; then I shall know fully, even as I am fully known." In this word picture, Paul revealed that our understanding of love is relational. He used this picture of engaging a person with an obstacle in the way. As long as that "poor reflection" is our understanding of that person, our relationship can only go so far. But once we are "face-to-face," our relationship can dive much deeper.

So our understanding of love is like a journey of learning, growing up, and deepening a relationship. What do all these things have in common? They all imply motion—moving, growing, and deepening. Paul seems to be telling us what love is and then telling us that love is a process that begins on earth, but is only fulfilled in eternity. After Paul challenged our motives, defined love clearly, and established that it is a life-long pursuit, he sealed the deal with the last verse, "And now these three remain: faith, hope and love. But the greatest of these is love."

These words have frustrated many of us. How can we choose among faith, hope, and love? They are core virtues—all critical to our relationship with Christ. What is God trying to tell us about our relationship to him?

Roberto and Carlos's story can be a useful analogy for understanding how faith, hope, and love work together as a unit. We are all in this life, which is represented by the sea. On our journey we have three tools—the boat, the chain, and the anchor—that help us move through life. In this picture the boat represents love, the chain represents hope, and the anchor represents faith.

Let's walk through this word picture to see how it illustrates how faith, hope, and love fit together in our understanding and experience of truth.

Truth from a Boat

Let's begin by looking at Roberto's perspective as he experienced truth from a boat. In the final verse of chapter thirteen, Paul listed three key forces in our relationship to God. For many Christians faith may seem to fit naturally with truth, but how does faith fit in with hope and love? Let's look to the sailing analogy to see these three forces in action.

Christ as the Seabed

Metaphorically, in our story of Roberto and Carlos, the seabed is Christ. The seabed is what allows an anchored boat to sway in the water safely. It is what gives the boat the ability to stay grounded in the storms. It is vast and expansive and does not change. In 1 Samuel 2:8, after God granted Hannah her improbable desire to have a son, she prayed, "For the foundations of the earth are the LORD's; upon them he has set the world."

The seabed is so vast; we will never know the entire depth and breadth of its character. The more we sail and the more we rely on the seabed, the more we will learn of it and the more we will trust it. So it is with our Savior. He is large and trustworthy and knowable, but we will never reach his ends.

Faith as the Anchor

The anchor that connects us to the seabed is our faith. The Greek words for *faith* represent the idea of moral conviction and reliance on the salvation that Jesus provides.[2] The anchor is those things we believe are true that connect us to the foundation—things like the Apostles' Creed and the Ten Commandments. This is where truth begins—but not where it ends. If truth's purpose ended with believing things to be true, then that truth would do us very little good in loving others. It would simply be a lump of lead sitting at the bottom of the ocean. An anchor is attached to something that allows it to be effective; and without that attachment, the anchor has no purpose.

Faith provides stability for the boat floating above. Without a strong faith underpinning our efforts to reach out in love to others, those efforts are without substance and may be done entirely with our own strength. Faith provides those tenets of conviction that help us decide how we will interact with the world around us and engage them with what we know to be true.

As with a boat, our anchor of faith provides safety as we navigate the circumstances of our lives. We know that no matter what happens to us on a daily basis, the God we have put our faith in has not changed. As our anchor of faith sinks into the seabed, our unchanging God takes hold of us and helps us to see more and more of who he is.

Hope as the Chain

Remember how Roberto was trying to get that anchor secured to the seabed? But what connected the anchor to his boat? It was the chain. Imagine that this represents our hope. This hope is our expectation and drive to be one with our Creator—to know him fully and to be fully known. This hope is connected to our faith—the anchor that manages all of the beliefs we have established as we have grown in our relationship with Christ.

The key to a fuller experience of truth has to do, in part, with the hope that connects faith to love. On one end, our hope is rooted in Christ and his revelation to us—the seabed. On the other end, our hope is connected to the boat, which represents our love. This chain of hope must firmly hold these two ends together.

The necessity of a strong chain is discovered during the turbulence we experience on our boats. The struggles we encounter test the strength of our chains, which connect our boats firmly to the seabed when the waters of our lives get choppy and challenging.

In fact, many of the issues with our truth lenses come as we try to understand our troubles and the world from God's perspective.

Through our struggles, the chain that holds the boat to the anchor is tested. The flexibility and strength of the chain allows for our boat to be buffeted by the winds and the waves and yet stay secured to the ocean bed. Hope holds us to what we know to be true.

In Hebrews 6 the author defined hope "as an anchor for the soul, firm and secure. It enters the inner sanctuary behind the curtain, where Jesus, who went before us, has entered on our behalf. He has become a high priest forever, in the order of Melchizedek." This verse gives us a fascinating picture—hope as the connection between the vast sea floor that is our Lord and Savior Jesus and the boat that represents our love.

The Greek words for *hope* speak to anticipation, expectation, and confidence.[3] Our hope unites our basic beliefs with our everyday lives. Hope is the passion to make our lives match those things we know about our Creator and our eternal salvation.

Love as the Boat

In our sailing analogy, Jesus is represented in the vast ocean floor; faith is the anchor that connects us to him; hope is the chain that ties the boat to the anchor; and finally the boat itself represents love. The boat is the most visible element. We see it buffeted by the waves and tossed by the wind. It is the object that is engaged in the world and that comes into contact with other boats.

No wonder Paul said that love is the most important. We cannot refuse to love—as we saw in the first verses of 1 Corinthians 13.

The key is that we cannot truly love unless we have an eternal hope and a solid faith. It is the culmination of faith, hope, and love in the real world of relationships, work, and family that creates an understanding of God's truth.

So if these three things are built and dependent on the person of Jesus Christ, then our definition of truth requires all three. This is the holistic model for truth that we present as the basis for this discussion about truth lenses. Truth requires our faith in what Jesus has said, our hope in his promises, and our obedience through love.

Truth is three dimensional—not flat. We learn in an environment that is dynamic and infinitely complex. In our human nature, we wish we could simply buy truth from a bookstore and consume it. However, as we dig into the Bible and build our relationship with Jesus, our experience with truth becomes more and more dynamic.

We gain more than just head knowledge. It may start there; but our minds are limited and we see through a glass darkly. Incorporating our knowledge of truth with hope in Christ gives us the ability to wait expectantly on Jesus to reveal more of himself to us. This process also includes our outward response to the knowledge and expectation in our daily lives—love. That response is the showcase of our faith and hope. When our response is centered in Christ, it is revealed as love. Paul stated it so well in Galatians 5:6, "The only thing that counts is faith expressing itself through love."

It is much like making cookies. We can have the recipe, telling us the ingredients and steps to make them, but the full truth or experience of making cookies is not in the recipe. We more completely understand what cookies are when we experience mixing the dough, waiting in expectation for them to bake, eating some of them, and sharing some with others. Our understanding goes far beyond mere ingredients. It includes smells (faith), desire (hope), and the look on a neighbor's face (love) when we share them graciously. All these parts combine to make the experience of cookies complete.

This means that when we talk about truth, we are talking about much more than a pile of things that we believe to be true. We are talking about the source of that truth, the actual elements themselves, and our obedience to them. If we are willing to look at truth in this way, it will mean a significant challenge for several reasons:

1. Truth becomes much more than information.
2. Truth begins to integrate with our purpose and actions.
3. Truth demands obedience, not simply understanding.
4. Truth leads to life transformation.

In John 8:31–32, Jesus said something that rocked the very foundation of the Jewish faith: "If you hold to my teaching, you are really my disciples. Then you will know the truth, and the truth will set you free." He says this in the context of being tested by the Pharisees, who brought before him an adulterous woman. They had verifiable testimony regarding the truth of her sin, and they wanted to trap him between this undeniable fact with its legal consequence and his love for the needy and helpless.

In an amazing turn of events, Jesus disarmed the challenge, and realizing they had been defeated, the Pharisees scattered. Out of that scenario many people were drawn to Jesus and believed in him. In those days the Jews had a saying "that no man was free, but he who exercised himself in the meditation of the law."[4] They had focused their understanding of God and his truth completely on the law.

As our pastor is fond of saying, Jesus interrupted their lives that day. In that interruption he expanded their concept of truth by his example. He allowed the Jews who were with him that day to see truth in a completeness that encompassed faith, hope, and love. And in that fresh demonstration of truth, Jesus offered life transformation.

Jesus never failed to expand the worlds and worldviews of those who believed in him. He does the same today. Jesus is the ultimate example of how faith, hope, and love come together. Through our relationship with Jesus Christ we come to know truth more fully. And this knowledge is guaranteed to transform us. What an amazing gift God's truth is. It is wisdom, expectation, and relationship all at the same time. We cannot even imagine how our lives will be changed as we allow the fullness of truth to impact our lives.

In the coming chapters, we will use this holistic way of looking at truth to help us think through different truth lenses and ask a simple question: Which lens will best help us understand the truth of God's character to be seen and lived out in our daily lives?

Chapter 7

HOLDING TRUTH LENSES UP TO THE BIBLE

L et's talk a bit more about the idea of holistic truth. We know that it is critical to have faith in what we know and hope in what God is doing, and to apply both of those things in love toward others. This may make sense, but it surely isn't easy. Many times we try to comprehend these three pieces, but our abilities are limited. We alternately focus on understanding faith or reaching out in love, forgetting about the other parts of the biblical directives. So we want to affirm the place of faith, hope, and love as we begin to hold each truth lens up to the Bible.

When we sat down with Dr. Hiebert to talk about this book, he challenged us to this task. He encouraged us to hold each truth lens up to the Bible and see which one best reflects the truth God is communicating to us. This is the next step in our thinking about what we think with and deciding if there are any assumptions we hold that do not fit with the Bible. So let us engage in this exercise

together as we are preparing to use these truth lenses to face challenges in our everyday lives.

The Power of Faith

Going back to our example of the sailboat off the Costa Rican
coast, we remember that the anchor is faith; and it is faith that
holds us to the seabed of truth, which represents Jesus Christ. For
the Rock Dwellers, who value truth highly, faith is the spiritual
dimension that they naturally gravitate toward because faith by
definition is deeply rooted in the truth.

Rock Dwellers see their job as truth delivery and persuasion.
They ask, "How can I help the most people to know and accept
the truth I have found?" In our culture we love tools, so it is easy
to think of the anchor of faith as the tool that allows us to connect
to the seabed of Christ. Rock Dwellers believe that through faith,
they will eventually know everything about the seabed.

Imagine a boat that has anchored in many parts of the same
small bay. That anchor has experienced much of the seabed in
that area. The more the boat travels, the more of the seabed is
understood. In the same way, positivists revel in being in the
seabed of God's Word, learning and experiencing the truth God
has revealed. Their desire is to eventually understand all they can
about God's Word and God's world.

The part of sailing that Rock Dwellers most look forward to
is setting the anchor—excited to learn more about the seabed each
time the anchor settles on it. This focus on the anchor (faith) is
very common with those who use the positivist truth lens. They
focus great attention on studying and understanding the Bible in

depth. They want to know what it really means, and they want to defend the truth they have added to their knowledge against untruth.

Holding firm to truth is a strong value in the Bible. In Ephesians 6:14 Paul wrote, "Stand firm then, with the belt of truth buckled around your waist, with the breastplate of righteousness in place." Truth is one of those armaments that allows us to persevere in the Christian walk. If we think about the purpose of a belt, it is what holds the whole outfit together. All the pieces that make up our equipment are centered around the belt.

In addition to understanding truth, Rock Dwellers feel a strong need to defend the truth. The idea of faith pictured as a strong metal anchor is inviting. They identify with a fierce defense of God's decrees and see strong verses in the Bible that affirm this. One of these verses that defends the truth and exactness of the Bible is Proverbs 30:5-8: "Every word of God is flawless; he is a shield to those who take refuge in him. Do not add to his words, or he will rebuke you and prove you a liar. Two things I ask of you, O LORD; do not refuse me before I die: Keep falsehood and lies far from me; give me neither poverty nor riches, but give me only my daily bread."

This admonition is very defined and specific. The author spoke about truth as something that is discoverable, understandable, and defined. These verses fit with how a positivist approaches truth. These words are adding up the truth of God's words and subtracting heresy.

Verses like these give Rock Dwellers confidence because they paint a picture of a God who expects us to respond to truth in exacting and clear ways. If God expects this of his people, then that must mean that he will make it possible.

Island Dwellers would struggle with the strong sentiment in these verses. Since truth is so personal, it would be hard to know when something another person says is a lie or simply part of his or her experience.

Island Dwellers stress God's compassion in order to help each person define faith in this very personal way. They believe that God wants to forgive and embrace people for who they are. They affirm passages like Joel 2:13 and interpret them personally, holding on to the promise of repentance and grace. "Rend your heart and not your garments. Return to the LORD your God, for he is gracious and compassionate, slow to anger and abounding in love, and he relents from sending calamity."

Because of the highly personal nature of faith within instrumentalism, justice and mercy become critical. Because Island Dwellers do not feel the same need to share their faith and ask others to consider it, their focus is on tolerance and love for others. They value how people are treated in the present. A powerful verse that represents this focus is Micah 6:8, "He has showed you, O man, what is good. And what does the LORD require of you? To act justly and to love mercy and to walk humbly with your God."

The Bible also presents God as a defined and clear presence—completely dependable and forever true. Numbers 23:19 says, "God is not a man, that he should lie, nor a son of man, that he should change his mind. Does he speak and then not act? Does he promise and not fulfill?" And 1 Samuel 15:29 says, "He who is the Glory of Israel does not lie or change his mind; for he is not a man, that he should change his mind."

The critical realist truth lens allows a person to gravitate equally to both types of verses about faith. Valley Dwellers can embrace the certainty of truth, while acknowledging that faith is lived out in flesh and blood experiences.

Ephesians 4:15 says, "But speaking the truth in love, we must grow up in every way into him who is the head, into Christ" (NRSV). Hiebert commented, "We need the hard love that compels us to speak the truth, and the hard truth that points us to Christ who so loved the world that he gave his life for it."[1] This view of faith remains a strong foundation on which Christians can build their lives in Christ and, at the same time, it gives room for that foundation to strengthen through ever-deepening relationships with Christ. Christian Valley Dwellers are freed to live out their faith, expressing the truth they know and realizing that there is truth they are learning. They are neither bound by the mandatory acceptance of all beliefs, as on the sandy islands, nor by the pressing need to have everyone agree, as on the rocky shore.

The far shore of the river where the Valley Dwellers live, with its humble belief that we are all in a process of learning, frames faith with the words of the writer of Hebrews, "Now faith is being sure of what we hope for and certain of what we do not see" (Hebrews 11:1). By putting faith in the context of hope, it validates what we know, but acknowledges the need to continue the search and to accept the mystery of life.

Flexible Hope

The wonderful thing about the chain of hope in our sailing analogy is that it makes connections. It is the combined strength of the anchor of faith and the chain of hope that keeps the boat from drifting. Valley Dwellers relate well with the analogy of the chain because it links together the essential elements.

Hope brings balance to the strong conviction of faith and the personal outpouring of love. It ties together knowable truth with personal perspective, making the system workable. Hope prompts Christians to grasp the strong truth verses with confidence and believe that they can be used in the messiness of day-to-day living.

The truth lens of critical realism is defined and understood in the chain that connects the anchor with the boat. This chain represents the hope we have in Christ as we are discovering the truth we are learning. The interesting thing about this truth lens is that its focus on the chain brings faith, hope, and love into a unity and holism that is not produced when viewing truth with either of the other truth lenses. By affirming the importance of the chain, Valley Dwellers understand the value of a strong faith foundation, but also see the importance of love and mercy.

A passage that explains the dynamic integration of these three is Hebrews 10:22-24: "Let us draw near to God with a sincere heart in full assurance of faith, having our hearts sprinkled to cleanse us from a guilty conscience and having our bodies washed with pure water. Let us hold unswervingly to the hope we profess, for he who promised is faithful. And let us consider how we may spur one another on toward love and good deeds." This integration brings strength to Valley Dwellers because it allows for faith, defines the context of hope in the future, and celebrates action in the form of love.

Rock Dwellers are most comfortable in faith and knowledge partly because they are such strong words in our language. On the other hand, the commonly used definition of *hope* in our culture seems weak. Phrases like "Here's hoping" and "I hope so" can make Rock Dwellers uncomfortable with the concept of hope, at first. It would be easy for a Rock Dweller to look at these verses and want to quickly move on to passages that use words like *knowledge* and *understanding*. But though the surface connotations of the word *hope* seem weak, the biblical meaning of the word is very strong. If Rock Dwellers go deeper to understand the biblical meaning of *hope*, they can then better understand the important interrelationships of faith, hope, and love that Paul was talking about.

As we discussed above, the biblical meaning of *hope* is an expectation of good, a joyful and confident expectation of eternal salvation. We think of a little girl's promised Christmas present wrapped under a tree. The child knows it is a doll; but she cannot hold the doll yet, and she does not know what its face will look like. She is sure that the promise is in the box, confident that she will get to open it on Christmas morning. Her hope is part of the experience of the doll. It is not just the knowledge of the doll that is important (faith), nor just the loving of the toy, but also the hopeful anticipation of a promise fulfilled.

If Rock Dwellers do not go on to understand this deeper meaning of hope, they may see hope as secondary to clear understanding, assuming that hope is an inadequate solution to uncertainty. In this mindset, the chain does not seem nearly as strong as the anchor that is imbedded in Christ. A Rock Dweller may wonder, *Why hope when you can know?* Rock Dwellers focus on knowing. This allows them to rely on their knowledge instead of hope. The words of Jesus in John 17:8 are a great encouragement to the Rock Dweller because there is great certainty: "For I gave them the words you gave me and they accepted them. They knew with certainty that I came from you, and they believed that you sent me."

Island Dwellers are most comfortable in the love and acceptance of those around them. To the Island Dwellers, the concept of hope seems futile because they assume that there is no knowable reality that can be agreed on. They hold out no hope because only their personal truth is significant. King Solomon struggled with this futility and lack of hope in Ecclesiastes 2:19-21, "And who knows whether he will be a wise man or a fool? Yet he will have control over all the work into which I have poured my effort and skill under the sun. This too is meaningless. So my heart began to despair over all my toilsome labor under the sun. For a man may do his work with wisdom, knowledge and skill, and then he must leave all he owns to someone who has not worked for it. This too is meaningless and a great misfortune."

So the chain of hope in our example is often ignored by both the Rock Dwellers and the Island Dwellers. Instead of understanding the interrelationships, hope seems overshadowed by either the depth of knowledge or the compassion of love.

Nature of Love

What is more powerful than a single act of love? Think about the last time someone did something loving and kind for you. It might have been a child bringing you a flower from the garden or a friend buying you coffee. Whatever it was, the impact was visible and lasting. That is the reality of the boat in our story. The boat is the most visible part of our analogy. It is the boat that gets rained on, that has to navigate around other boats, and that is stepped on; but the boat might just save a life in a rescue. It is the interactive piece of our story.

Island Dwellers view the world from the boat. Because truth is very personal, the unseen anchor doesn't seem as important as what happens on the boat. In the minds of most Island Dwellers, the anchor is a personal connection to God and is useful only to the extent that it holds their lives to the seabed. In this way, the main focus becomes what is happening on the boat—loving others and allowing them to have their own personal connections to God.

The Bible speaks often about love and about the endless forgiveness of Christ. Island Dwellers grab on to verses like 1 Peter 4:8: "Above all, love each other deeply, because love covers over a multitude of sins." This aspect of God's love touches Island Dwellers deeply. It allows them to leave to God the whole matter of sin and its effects. This leaves them free to love people and trust that God will work with each person individually.

All boats bob in the water and have different experiences. It is the boat that allows people to love and connect with each other. When Island Dwellers read the Bible, they gravitate toward the love verses, because they see their job primarily as loving others. Making judgments or learning more hard truth is seen as secondary or counterproductive to the really important work of interacting with others, since any discoveries are seen as nontransferable anyway. Romans 13:8–10 might resonate well with this truth lens because it focuses on loving others, which fulfills the law: "Let no debt remain outstanding, except the continuing debt to love one another, for he who loves his fellowman has fulfilled the law. The commandments, 'Do not commit adultery,' 'Do not murder,' 'Do not steal,' 'Do not covet,' and whatever other commandment there may be, are summed up in this one rule: 'Love your neighbor as yourself.' Love does no harm to its neighbor. Therefore love is the fulfillment of the law."

Many Rock Dwellers see love for their neighbors as best demonstrated by presenting truth to them clearly and helping them to see the right way. They use the phrase "truth in love," in Ephesians 4:15 to describe a style of delivering truth, not necessarily as action in other's lives. In the same way, hope is seen as a means to help them deliver the truth with certainty. In the world of the Rock Dweller, the anchor of faith becomes more important than either the chain or the boat.

One of the verses a person with a positivist truth lens would point to is James 1:6-8: "But when he asks, he must believe and not doubt, because he who doubts is like a wave of the sea, blown and tossed by the wind. That man should not think he will receive anything from the Lord; he is a double-minded man, unstable in all he does." Rock Dwellers are intimidated or even threatened by the waves crashing against the boat. They find their comfort and security in the anchor, because the boat itself is unstable and uncertain. They don't know what may come their way. Other boats, islands, sharks, or weather are seen as threats or necessary evils. Interacting with the world through this truth lens can seem guarded with a mindset that is most interested in security and safety, because the evils of the world are out there and are scary. Others meet these threats as opportunities to engage the world with the truth their anchor provides. However, this is not necessarily in line with the goal of loving others, but of showing love on the condition that others accept the truth they deliver.

The Valley Dwellers experience faith, hope, and love as a working unit, with love being the outward expression of their faith walk and their hope in what Christ is doing in their lives. For them the boat is an opportunity to both love others and learn together by building relationships. Learning builds their understanding of each other and how God is working in the lives of his people.

Valley Dwellers interact with the world without the fear of coming loose from their anchor. Their truth of Christ and his Word empowers them to love others. They can feel secure, knowing their anchor will hold firm, hoping in what God will do, and then seeing what God does through them as they interact with the world.

Ephesians 4:14-16 describes the security they walk in: "Then we will no longer be infants, tossed back and forth by the waves, and blown here and there by every wind of teaching and by the cunning and craftiness of men in their deceitful scheming. Instead, speaking the truth in love, we will in all things grow up into him who is the Head, that is, Christ. From him the whole body, joined and held together by every supporting ligament, grows and builds itself up in love, as each part does its work."

All three truth lenses see different passages of the Bible as having great significance. Not that they deny the truth of the other passages, but certain sections resonate more strongly within them.

During our talks with Dr. Hiebert, he encouraged us to bear witness to what the far shore of the river might look like. What we discovered is that living in the valley allows the Christian to see these verses as a working unit to help us know Christ through humility, hope in what he will accomplish in the world, and love others as an outpouring of that faith and hope.

We see this in Paul's prayer in Philippians 1:9-11: "And this is my prayer; that your love may abound more and more in knowledge and depth of insight, so that you may be able to discern what is best and may be pure and blameless until the day of Christ, filled with the fruit of righteousness that comes through Jesus Christ—to the glory and praise of God."

This is just the first step of the exercise of looking at our truth lenses in light of the Bible. We challenge you to continue thinking about how your assumptions about truth affect how you live out your faith in your day-to-day life and relationships. Our prayer is that the Holy Spirit will teach you as you study the Bible.

Chapter 8

THE GREAT DISTURBANCE

I n River Town everyone is on a journey. Imagine the town full of activity. There is a man on a rock, climbing down toward the beach. A child is standing on the beach, throwing pebbles into the water. Others are swimming hard across the current. A man on the sand suddenly stands and gets into the water. A woman on the far side is making a visit to the rocky side. Now imagine where you might fit into this scene.

Peter Kreeft said in his book The Journey that the first decision we make is whether or not to travel.[1] Some people in River Town have decided not to travel. They are comfortable with how they view truth, and they are comfortable with where they live.

Defining Disturbances

A great disturbance occurs when a truth lens cannot bring into focus a certain truth that we encounter—when things don't make sense. This immediately brings a sense of disequilibrium and dissonance. These events can be upsetting and concerning, or they can be moments for new ideas and inspiration. For instance, internal discord may occur in a situation that seems unjust and we are not sure why, or it may be brought on by a strained relationship that we can't seem to fix. This dissonance can also come to life through a major breakthrough or innovation. Many different situations may create disturbances.

Disturbances are part of life, and most are resolved by our current truth lens. There may be circumstances that are new or different in our lives that our truth lens cannot help us resolve. But when the truth lens is out of focus and does not provide a reasonable understanding of this new truth, then our lens is challenged, creating a great disturbance. When a truth we know bumps into a new truth we can't deny, we experience disequilibrium; and a door is opened to evaluate our truth lens. This is just the opportunity we need in our desire to attain a more biblical worldview.

Disturbances are personal; they can be triggered by relationships or people who make choices informed by a different truth lens. Because others may come to their conclusions in a different way, our hearts and minds may become disturbed. When an issue is theoretical, it is easier to take a decisive stand. But often during a moment of dissonance, we have a face, a name, and a bond with a person who is looking at the world differently, and we may desperately want to reconcile the difference. But when we look at their actions, they seem out of focus; and the same is probably true when they look at us. So we struggle to work through the validity of others' choices in light of our own truth lenses.

Disturbances are emotional. Each time our world is interrupted, we are buffeted by fear, defensiveness, isolation, excitement, and a million other feelings that hit us like so many raindrops. These emotions crest because we are being challenged deep within. When our truth lens is not sufficient to deal with a major issue, it is unsettling and unnerving. We always thought that our truth lens would be enough to guide us through anything life could throw at us, but sometimes a disturbance happens, and important assumptions are swept away.

Let's take some simple examples of disturbances to illustrate this point. The examples we have chosen are not nearly as complex as many real life situations, because we want to provide you with a starting place from which you can begin to understand the great disturbances in your own life in light of your truth lens.

Disturbances for Rock Dwellers

Because of the growing pluralism in our world where Christianity is regularly challenged, people with a truth lens like a Rock Dweller have to deal with disturbances almost on a daily basis. Let's look at three different scenarios and strategies for dealing with disturbances.

Pride and Loving Others

A positivist, or a Rock Dweller, is describing a situation at work. The people in his workplace consider him a very intolerant religious conservative. Their attitude bothers him because, though he holds his views very dear, he also loves the people around him. He doesn't agree with the values and decisions of their lives, but mostly he tries to stay quiet unless he's asked his opinion. But being quiet is an effort. He likes to be right. He often feels compelled to debate with others, trying to bring them around to his views.

This Rock Dweller-type loves a debate. Winning is not only fun, but necessary to defend the truth. Without the fight, the truth may slide down the slippery slope of relativism and our world will continue to decline. There are many different motivations behind the fight. One can be pride. The goal is being right, not learning or bringing the other person to a point of change. Another motivation is fear, fear of losing moral and rational bearings. Truth will fall away and the world of right and wrong will disappear (going into the river). When positivism is questioned, the frightening thought comes, What will happen if the truth I know turns out to be false?

Then Christ begins to work in this person's life, teaching him to show his love to others. Over time he realizes that being right and winning a fight isn't the most important thing. He should love others. At these difficult moments, he reminds himself to "be the bigger person" and "take the high road." God is beginning to change his view of truth. But avoiding conflict is a constant struggle. When he doesn't stand up for the truth, he feels good about loving others and bad about not defending the truth. When he stands strong for the truth, he somehow feels he is putting the other person second. So, how can he love others and still believe there is a right and wrong?

Some people feel this disturbance and look for ways to make the truth they know work together with their desire to reach out to others. It bothers them when they cannot leverage these two forces together. When the rocky pile of truth does not allow them to love those around them, they begin to wonder why this truth isn't a better tool. It causes a sense of helplessness and frustration in which the person can't seem to take the truth they know and apply it to helping others.

This sense of helplessness is the moment of opportunity. While there are many responses that people will consider, most of us either begin looking for another perspective on truth or retreat into the solace of the truth that we are sure about. If we do retreat from this disturbance we may even sacrifice relationships or opportunities to reach out in an effort to maintain our hold on the truth—in order to be right. On the other hand, if we accept the disturbance as a real dilemma, we will begin to factor the role of relationships into our understanding of truth. Most likely, we will begin this search as we do most of our truth gathering, through study and research that will give us formulas and strategies to see the disturbance through our current truth lens.

Fear and the Unknowable

A student is studying late for her first test in her ethics class at a private college far from home. All week while listening to her professor laying out the different strategies for evaluating ethical behavior, she felt like there was a rock in her stomach. How could there be so many options about what is ethical? She was always taught that all we need is the Bible to decide right and wrong, and now that didn't seem sufficient.

From the first day of class, the professor had focused on the fact that what people believe to be right and wrong is not anything that can be written in a simple list. It is complex, factoring in culture, environment, and history. Over and over he described real-life situations that could not be ethically solved easily using her truth lens. This new reality of the unknown bothered her deeply and she couldn't get her mind off the implications in her own life. She always believed in an absolute set of right and wrong that she had been taught as she grew up. Always the good debater, she was frustrated that in ethics class she could not come up with the right argument to make her case.

Finally, one rainy evening, she sat in front of her dorm window with her ethics book on her desk and threw the book on the floor in desperation. She had come to a point where she thought she had to either reject everything her professor was saying or agree that there are things that are unknowable.

What has she just experienced? A great disturbance. Her logical mind racing, she began to see that her logic was bringing her closer and closer to the river's edge. Truth was not as black and white as she always thought. As her feet began to get wet in our river, she felt a wave of disequilibrium sweep over her. She decided to retreat to the rocks and completely reject what the professor proposed in class. Maybe next semester she would take physics instead.

Control and the Proof

William Wilberforce made it his life goal to see slavery abolished in the British Empire. For years he argued in the British Parliament to end slave trade, but the power of the slavers was significant. With so many parliamentary members invested in the plantations around the world that used slaves, it was a battle that seemed impossible to win.

One of his key efforts was to prove what the slave conditions were like and how many of the slaves were dying on their initial trips from Africa. As he gathered this data, he built his argument. At the same time, his adversaries in government built opposing arguments designed to question his proof. Wilberforce wanted control of the parliament in order to pass his bill. For that he had to have proof that would earn him that control.

We do the same on a daily basis. We are always vying for control of situations in our lives for many reasons—good and bad. As we do this we bring proof that our solution is the right one and should earn the respect and following of others. If our solution is adopted, we gain control.

In positivism, the disturbance happens when people build their cases and pile up the truth to a convincing size, but then something unexplainable occurs. That huge pile of truth does not win the day. Instead, control is awarded based on another set of criteria entirely. Maybe the people are looking at truth from an instrumentalist truth lens, and they are making their judgments based on how usable the answers are or how they promote relationships.

Whatever the case, this is a moment of trauma because all the efforts to convince people of a fact based on proof do not work. At this moment Rock Dwellers must make a choice. Will they continue to work under the model of gaining control by gathering evidence, or will they look to another truth lens?

Disturbances for Island Dwellers

Life on the sandy islands allows for individual freedom of thought. In this environment, people have room to explore and enjoy their thoughts and their ideas. However, there may come a time when they will look for something to help them escape the doubt in their lives. Out of this dynamic come great disturbances. Island Dwellers also have a variety of strategies for dealing with disturbances. Let's take a deeper look at three of them.

Relationship and Resolution

The young couple takes long walks in the park at least once a week. The dark green canopy of leaves provides an amazing array of dancing sun beams that play tag with their feet as they walk along briskly. This park is a special place. They met here and he proposed here. So as they walk, it is only natural to imagine the conversations they might have about their lives, their dreams, and their experiences.

They are the sort of couple who decided early on that arguing about issues would not be part of their love. Instead, they would accept their differences and enjoy their relationship without the disagreement. This special love refused to talk about politics, religion, or any other divisive force. It focused only on their shared experiences and their passion for life. And so they lived.

Then one day *the decision* rose up and it stopped them in their spirited tracks. They had always said that they would live in the city near this park where they walked so often. It was a pact they had made. But then a job offer came and the wife wanted them to move to a small rural town near a large business complex. The job was incredible—what she had always dreamed of.

And so they were stuck. On one hand, they had made a promise to live in the city, but, on the other hand, she had an incredible job offer in the country. Both options were valid and important. But in a relationship where experience reigned and the individual was isolated, they had no mechanism to cope with this.

And so they walked without saying a word, unable to even discuss what to do.

This example illustrates a powerful disturbance in the lives of Island Dwellers. As they develop relationships in the river, they do not develop ways to make significant decisions in conflict. So when two friends, co-workers, family members, or a couple who live with this truth lens come to major decisions that cannot be personalized, then their lives are disturbed. In this moment someone has to be *right* or *favored* or *more valued*, but there is no established criterion to resolve such conflicts and determine what is right. In this conflict the islands have no bridges when they desperately need them.

We all encounter difficult situations. The situation could be whether to allow your teenager to get a tattoo like her friends. Or you could have to decide between going to the Lutheran church that you grew up in or the Baptist church that your spouse grew up in. Maybe it is a moment when you have to decide what you will teach your children about the evolution/creation debate. Any of these might be a disturbance that causes you to take stock of your truth lens and ask how it can help you navigate a very challenging issue.

Cause and Self

She was volunteering at the local homeless shelter and started out going only one afternoon a month. However, the place got its hooks into her and soon she was on the steering committee, surrounded by a group of people who felt passionate about helping the local homeless people in the community. She loved the cause and the work being done. It gave her a sense of purpose and meaning.

One day at a steering committee meeting, the chairperson made a comment about the lack of volunteers. As the conversation progressed and the emotions escalated, the groups made a pledge to each try and recruit five volunteers over the next few months. As she left the meeting that day, she ran into a good friend. She had known this friend for years, but they hardly agreed on anything. That had always been okay because his beliefs were his own concern.

When she asked her friend to be a volunteer, he looked at her quizzically, then looked down at his shoes—obviously embarrassed about his feelings. The air filled with umms, ahhhs, and excuses right out of a playbook. She left feeling discouraged. How could her friend whom she cared so much about be so unconcerned? Could she continue to be his friend if he didn't care enough about others to give some time to help? What kind of person would not be willing to help? Her truth lens was being stretched as she strove to understand why her good friend had no interest in such an important cause.

Her passion created a crack in her instrumentalist truth lens. Without realizing it, she had allowed herself to believe in something that she expected others to embrace. When she tried to share what she believed with her friend and was rejected, it surprised her and she felt hurt. In the past she hadn't cared if someone disagreed with her values. It surprised her that she cared about what others thought about her new cause.

Community Impact and freedom

A young man lives at home and goes to community college. It's not that he doesn't want to go out of state for school, but his mother is very sick, and his dad is working long hours. Sometimes the young man helps his mom with some of the housework or makes supper, and other times his dad is able to help. The family had never talked about this arrangement. It seemed to just happen as the mother became disabled.

He usually just let life happen, but when a scholarship to a school out of state became available, something made him jump at the chance. He filled out the paperwork and waited with excitement. This might be just the opportunity to jumpstart his life. And then came the day of the letter. He opened it and everything about it was a big YES!

But when he told his parents, they became agitated. They tried to show excitement, but his dad especially looked crushed; and it dawned on him what his father was thinking. How could his father take care of everything alone? The son felt frustrated because he wanted to do what was best for his future. Wasn't college a good thing? Shouldn't his parents be thrilled for him? But they weren't, and this was a moment of disturbance.

Will the instrumentalist truth lens that defines the truth based on personal reality be enough to guide him through this situation? Will he have to consider another lens in order to make this decision in a way that honors him and also his parents?

One of the strong pillars of instrumentalism is the freedom that comes from a personal reality that does not bow to pressure from outside forces. Since we are all born egocentric, the freedom to do and think the way we please makes the most sense to us.

This provides a strong incentive to adopt the instrumentalist truth lens. As we live out our beliefs and convictions, however, there are moments when our freedom is challenged.

As long as a person's reality only impacts his or her own life, it is easier to keep from being disturbed. But the minute a person's reality and decisions affect someone else, there is the potential for a disturbance. It is likely to happen simply because the freedom that results from living on the islands does not anticipate how the ripples will affect others.

Instrumentalists have three options when they are confronted with a great disturbance. They can regroup and remind themselves that everyone's truth is personal and that they shouldn't care about what others decide to believe in, staying on the sandy beaches. They can take this feeling of truth and swim back to the rocky shore to begin building their rock pile once again on the foundation of positivism. Or, they can swim on to the far shore, hoping for a solution.

Disturbances for Valley Dwellers

The truth lens of critical realism is a relatively new way of looking at truth. It's hard to know what types of great disturbances Valley Dwellers will experience. In looking at critical realism and the community in the valley, we hope for a more biblical truth lens. However, Valley Dwellers should be open to continuing their journey of learning about how God views truth. Great disturbances play a role in this learning process, perhaps even inspiring people to venture on into the mountains where new communities might be established.

During difficult times the pragmatism and personal intuition on the sandy islands may look inviting to the Valley Dweller, because finding answers through critical realism takes time, energy, and cooperation among people. It may be tempting at times to revert to positivism with its ability to put knowledge into silos so conflicts can be left alone.

The great disturbances we talk about with positivism and instrumentalism have to do the role logic plays in daily life. The disturbances that arise for Valley Dwellers deal more with how they explore and understand all the different ways of knowing. Valley Dwellers often have disturbances, but because the truth lens is designed to deal with them, they don't always become great disturbances that challenge the assumption about truth. The following is an example of a disturbance that can happen with a critical realist truth lens.

It is a very embarrassing thing, but it happens more often than we would like to admit. We might be at a new house or simply disoriented and we miss a doorway and run right into the wall. Or picture a sitcom in which a house or restaurant has a swinging door. This type of door usually swings out when pushed, allowing a person to pass through. But if someone is standing on the other side of the door, it doesn't swing and stops the person pushing it. In this way, it acts more like a wall. When this happens on television, someone is usually carrying a large platter of food or a very breakable item.

Discerning what is a wall and what is a door is important to getting around. It is helpful to remember the phrase *the truth you know and the truth you are learning*. Valley Dwellers often encounter situations that reveal *the truth they are learning*. This is a disturbance, but not a great one. They know that this situation may be a wall or a door with someone on the other side. They push carefully, knowing that their knowledge is not complete.

Let's say that you have established respect for life as a truth you know. That becomes a wall for you that is stable and dependable. You find that as you meet more people from other cultures and expand your learning, this truth is validated—a wall is found firm. However, what often happens is that when the next issue surfaces, you then make some seemingly natural mental jump into another area and expect to encounter a wall. But sometimes as you push on it, you find that it is really a door opening to an area of truth that you are learning.

Let's say that this mental jump involves the elephants of Africa. The value of life is a wall for you, and as you learn more about the elephants that are being massacred for their tusks, you take a strong position on their preservation. But one day you watch an interview with a poacher. You find out that his family is starving because of war and poverty in his country and he must find a way to keep them alive. He hated to kill the elephants but reasoned that his family was more important than the life of the elephant. You just ran into a door that you thought was a wall.

This is a moment of disturbance. You work from the *truth you know* and you find out that, actually, it is *truth you are learning*. At this moment of disequilibrium, you will be tempted to not pursue this truth and go back to the islands or cross back to the rocky shore and take a definitive stand. This dilemma will challenge your truth lens and your desire to learn. With time, patience, and hard work, you will be able to harmonize portions of the truth you know and the truth you are learning.

You may not be able to resolve all the conflicts in your knowledge, but you realize that you can live with some dissonance while on the journey of discovery. This sense that it is possible to harmonize what you are learning resolves the disturbance enough to allow you to keep going. However, if one of those ingredients is taken away, the decision becomes harder. For instance, if you are presented with the opportunity to give to two organizations—one reaching out to the families of people like the poacher and one that is trying to save the elephants—it becomes much harder to make a quick decision. Positivism and instrumentalism offer quicker solutions, and during times of dissonance a Valley Dweller may think about returning to the sandy islands.

Necessary Disturbances

It sounds crazy, but it's true: we need these disturbances. While they are inconvenient, frustrating, time-consuming, and disorienting, we cannot grow without them. Each disturbance in life will do one of two things:

1. Through the struggle, our truth lenses will grow, and we will better understand what we think with.
2. Through the struggle, we will realize that our truth lenses are not adequate to help us come to a resolution, and we will consider changing our lenses to meet this struggle with more success.

It is often difficult to look at a challenge as an opportunity. In fact, we usually roll our eyes at that language because it has become such a cliché. We relegate it to a poster in the office or a trite quote in our e-mail signature. But before it was overused, it was describing something worth considering. Each disturbance will be a painful experience that not only rocks our boat but also gives us a significant opening to reconsider how we approach truth. One thing that a disturbance does without fail is get our attention. It grabs us by the shoulders and insists on being our focus. Hopefully, we will take advantage of that focus and think about how our truth lenses affect our interpretations of what we see.

What a great opportunity! That might sound painful if you are reading this while in the vise grip of a disturbance. But you don't want to allow these events to defeat you. This is where hope comes into the picture. As you recall from our nautical analogy of truth from a boat, the hope is what connects our turbulent lives to the anchor of our faith. It keeps us secure during these challenges and allows us to draw from our faith based on our circumstances.

These great disturbances have contributed to human history. Great examples of this are the songs that make up our faith. One of the most powerful hymns about hope testifies to the author's understanding that the struggles of life can only be survived because there is an anchor in Jesus Christ:

> My hope is built on nothing less
> Than Jesus' blood and righteousness;
> I dare not trust the sweetest frame,
> But wholly lean on Jesus' name.
> On Christ, the solid Rock, I stand;
> All other ground is sinking sand.
> — "My Hope Is Built on Nothing Less,"
> Edward Mote, 1797–1874

Disturbing Interactions

Another result of these great disturbances is discussion. As we ponder the song above, we might imagine that the author wrote these words after many late-night talks with friends, teachers, mentors, parents, and even strangers. When our lives are disturbed, we seek answers. We look outside ourselves and see if others might be able to help us get through our challenges.

In these discussions we come face to face with people who may have a different truth lens than we do. We hear their advice and are introduced to their thought processes. A great example of disequilibrium in the Bible is the story of Job. Job experienced profound loss and disturbance beyond anything we have probably known. As he was sitting there decimated in body, mind, and spirit, his friends came to console him. Each of them interpreted Job's problem through a truth lens of his own.

As Job listened to his friends, prayed to God, and considered the situation, he received different interpretations. In the end, the disturbance caused him to take a great step of faith and believe in his God against his friends' advice and common sense. But would he have come to that conclusion if he had not had his friends representing the other options?

The story of Job is a good warning. When we are in the middle of our disturbance, the people we interact with may give us the wrong advice. In these moments of weakness, it is easy to take the wrong direction. The strength of our anchor's connection to the seabed—Jesus Christ—will be critical for us to evaluate all of the interactions and discern wisdom.

Being Open to Challenge

As we've described these disturbances, a pattern has appeared. When the assumptions we hold—those *things we think with*—hold us back from accepting the truth the Holy Spirit reveals to us through the Bible, we have a disturbance. It is in these times that no matter what truth lens we hold, we need to be open to allowing our assumptions to be challenged. In this way, our assumptions and our understanding of God and his world will continually come closer and closer to the truth until we are with God someday and no longer see through a glass darkly.

So now that we have thought through these disturbances and how they affect us, let's walk through some practical issues that will allow us to see how our truth lenses impact our lives.

Chapter 9

TRUTH LENSES AND RELATIONSHIPS

et's imagine that there is a family in River Town with members living in all three communities. They started out on the rocky shore all together, but soon some of the family decided to join those living out on the islands. Then a couple of the family members swam to the far shore. However, just because they have settled in different communities doesn't mean they don't love to gather as all families do. They get together for picnics, holidays, and birthdays—enjoying each other's company.

But in the midst of the barbeques on the sandbar, the Christmas Eve celebrations on the rocky shore, and the surprise birthday parties on the far shore, there are challenges to their relationships as they strive to relate using different truth lenses. It is in these moments of challenge that they often wish for the days when they all lived in the same community and used the same truth lens. It was easier to enjoy their times together then.

Entering Relationships

At their core, relationships are created by factors such as trust, intimacy, and like-mindedness. As people are drawn together in work environments or in their neighborhoods, they begin to subconsciously size each other up to see if there are any natural affinities. This process is hard to describe because it happens so naturally.

One of the subconscious check boxes that we have when we are getting to know others has to do with truth lenses. As we talk and share stories, common experiences, and opinions, we are trying to see if other people look at the world the same way we do. One of the things we do when we interact with them is listen for clues that give insight into their truth lens. We may be listening for definitive and decisive language. Another person may be seeing how open-minded we are in our opinions and thoughts. Another key indicator is what people want to talk about. As we hear about the causes, interests, and passions of a person, we begin to understand how that person interacts with the world and how he or she views truth.

We gravitate toward people who share our view of truth, and these relationships often develop naturally. But many times as people begin to relate, their differing truth lenses cause disagreements. These early flare-ups can easily destroy relationships, and people move on to relate with those who see the world in more complementary ways.

Of course, there are people who enjoy relating to others who think differently. These people may even gravitate toward different points of view because they hold this as a value. There are also those relationships we can't escape—relationships formed at work or at school when we are assigned to work with someone who sees the world differently. And most commonly, family gatherings bring together people who have many different viewpoints.

So even as we strive to build relationships with those who are like us, we live in a world where we must relate with many different people on a daily basis.

Communicating from a Truth Lens

There are certain phrases that will inform us about someone's underlying truth lens. Those with a positivist truth lens frame their interactions in terms of universal principles. They tend to speak very definitively and confidently. Many Rock Dwellers don't use phrases such as "I think" or "I see it this way." Instead, they speak as though the things they believe represent universal principles, not mere opinion.

People using the instrumentalist truth lens often talk in first-person pronouns. We will hear many references to their personal experiences and their journeys. Although very willing to give their opinions and interact, these Island Dwellers will be less argumentative and more accommodating.

People using the critical realist truth lens are known to speak using analogy. They are more likely to use phrases such as "we are considering," "we are learning," or "you might think about it this way." They speak of process rather than end results or goals. This is often framed by saying things like, "We are working toward a better understanding of . . ." While they will interact and defend positions that they believe in, they will allow for the possibility that they do not have the full picture yet.

When Rock Dwellers speak with Valley Dwellers, things usually start well because they both value identifying and discovering truth. However, as they begin to dive into a topic, the Rock Dweller may begin to get frustrated because the Valley Dweller is not talking about truth as a static reality, but as a process. The Rock Dweller is looking to establish undeniable principles and feels as though the Valley Dweller is dodging the real issue or is not willing to take a hard enough stand.

When an Island Dweller speaks with a Rock Dweller, the conversations are usually rather short or turn to superficial themes very quickly. This is because the Island Dweller is looking to develop a relationship around common experiences, while the Rock Dweller is looking to find someone who is interested in building rock piles. The Island Dweller will not feel comfortable forcing the issue of finding truth that they both can know. This effort may seem like a waste of time for the Island Dweller, but the Rock Dweller has no choice but to keep pushing the issue to get resolution.

When a Valley Dweller is talking with an Island Dweller, they will both see the value of their personal knowledge and can have engaging conversations about these very personal ideas and experiences. They will both feel comfortable with the language about *experience* and *journey*. But these relationships will probably not go very deep because the Valley Dweller will feel that the Island Dweller can't take that next step toward discovering truth together. However, Valley Dwellers are likely to hold out hope for this common learning process. They will desire to journey together, but the Island Dweller will most likely not see the value of this and will disengage.

For English speakers, one of the challenging parts of communicating between truth lenses is that much of the English language is riddled with either/or words that originated on the rocky shore. So, even if you hold a different truth lens, you have to work with the words and phrases everyone knows. This means that when Island Dwellers say, "We disagree," they are describing the fact that two people cannot precisely share what they know. It also means that the Rock Dweller believes that people using other truth lenses are skirting issues or not speaking to the question, because the question itself does not make sense in the other truth lens. They may describe people as wishy-washy when they refuse to phrase things the way the language naturally prompts them to speak.

Conflict in Relationships

We can't blame every conflict or relationship challenge on truth lenses. There are many reasons why people have challenges in their relationships. Some are based on conflicting personalities and others are based on spiritual issues. Sometimes we fight and debate about truth when the real issue is that we just don't like someone. On the surface it looks like we are fighting because we disagree, but actually the source of our conflict is another issue entirely. However, many conflicts in relationships do stem from our truth lenses. We each see the world a certain way, and many of us have the expectation that others should see it the same way. However, we are often confronted with the fact that they don't.

By having the ability to distinguish between a conflict that is based on a truth lens difference and other kinds of conflicts, we can choose to discuss issues about our truth lenses when that is the root problem.

Let's take some time to explore how different people deal with truth lens conflicts so we can try to find ways to build bridges between the gaps in our beliefs about truth.

Agreeing to Agree

For Rock Dwellers, friendships will tend to rise and fall based on how much of the picture puzzles they are putting together matches the puzzles of others. If personal efforts to add truth and subtract untruth are in line with a friend's efforts, then a Rock Dweller will find a comfortable connection. However, if personal pictures don't match, the challenges will be much greater. The positivist truth lens does not facilitate relating to those who disagree. For the most part, Rock Dwellers will have to either ignore differences or face them head on and try to resolve the ambiguity. Hiebert explained, "The naturalistic view works well in the physical sciences, but it faces a problem in studying humans. Either it must reduce them to material objects, like other objects, or it must admit their subjectivity and, therefore, an inability to truly know them. There's little room for intersubjective human communication or for people to reveal their inner beliefs and feelings."[1]

The challenge with these two options is that one is very superficial and may not last. The other requires confrontation of the untruth in a friend's decision, lifestyle, or understanding. Then both individuals will either see truth the same way or reject the relationship.

While the idea of adding truth and subtracting untruth sounds very simple, doing the same with other people becomes very complex—even messy. How many times have you heard friends describe their time with family at the holidays like this: "They are so off base I don't even bother to talk about what I am going through. We just talk about food and football"? Or you might have heard something like this: "I got in an argument with my cousin again. I can't understand him at all. When I tried to talk sense into him, all we did was fight."

Hiebert described this dynamic: "Positivism is characterized by attacks and counterattacks as each party claims to have the truth."[2] The natural result is that Rock Dwellers are attracted to those who are on a similar truth search. They develop strong groups around their picture puzzle and focus their time and relationships there.

Agreeing to Disagree

You may have been jumping forward in your mind to some of the interesting consequences of having the instrumentalist truth lens. The most striking is that there is no way to affirm a larger truth that applies to everyone. This truth lens is laid out in striking contrast to the positivist truth lens in that it completely gives up on the idea that all truth is knowable.

Once you have seen the world through this truth lens for a time, the natural result is a strong sense of pragmatism. This deeply affects your relationships. This happens for some very simple reasons. If you and those around you don't have a common set of truth, then what you believe must be something that benefits you. And if it is to serve only you, then you tend to select something that is personally convenient and helpful to your vision of what life should be like.

Let's consider an example. One day you wake up and it dawns on you that the passion you used to have for your spouse is gone. You tell your spouse, "I want something more for my life than what you can give me." As you stumble down the stairs for your morning coffee, you realize that your marriage is over. For you, given the place you find yourself, there is nothing wrong with getting a divorce. As you begin to feel more comfortable with the idea of divorce, you may not even consider what your spouse is feeling because that is not your concern, after all.

Some time later you get a call from your spouse. Over the phone you hear the crying of a frustrated and sad person who says, "I thought we believed that divorce is wrong? What about 'till death do us part?'" You simply respond, "I know how you feel, but where I am at personally, divorce is what I have to do."

In chapter four we talked about the useful fictions that help Island Dwellers make decisions. These useful fictions are essential to relationships with people using the instrumentalist truth lens. In the example we used above, the big question in the mind of the spouse asking for the divorce was not, Is the concept of divorce an acceptable solution? Instead, the fundamental question was, Can my personal view of divorce support my desire to separate from my spouse?

Agreeing to Learn Together

The distinctive response of Valley Dwellers in a disagreement is in what they do not do and do not say. Because they live in a posture of learning where the lack of certainty does not cripple them, they do not necessarily begin by questioning the foundational assumptions of the person they are disagreeing with. Instead, a person using the critical realist truth lens will take into account the person, the culture, the idea, and the context of the discussion. With that broad consideration underway, Valley Dwellers will then compare what is being said to the foundation of the truth they know. If the theme or topic does not contradict the truth they know, then they begin to ask how they can learn from this different perspective. If the idea presented does contradict the truth they know, Valley Dwellers will consider whether their understanding of truth should be expanded or whether they must continue processing the idea.

Let's explore this through a real-life example. Imagine you have a leadership role in a church that has always had a very traditional style of worship. In fact, the music style was one of the reasons that your family chose to attend this church. You enjoy it and believe it is an appropriate way to honor God. Then the church calls a new pastor, and he decides that he would like to blend worship styles to connect with different audiences. When you first hear of this idea, you immediately bristle. You know what happens when churches go down this path.

So you set up a meeting with the pastor and over coffee you begin to talk. You lay out your opinion and share some Bible passages that you believe affirm what you are presenting. He then very kindly does the same. So you begin to ask questions and engage each other more deeply about the subject. You establish the truth you know about worship, and in the discussion you realize that the new pastor has some ideas that resonate with that. By the end of your meeting, you both have affirmed each other's core beliefs and have learned more about worship. You have gained a greater appreciation for worship that connects with a younger generation, and your pastor can express a better understanding of the holiness of God in worship. In that meeting you established a mutual respect and understanding that will facilitate solutions as the pastor's ideas about worship are implemented.

In this way, Valley Dwellers tend to enjoy more peaceful relationships with people. Even when they see others doing and believing things that they disagree with, they can rest, knowing that God is in control. They do not always feel compelled to defend God's truth in every setting or circumstance, knowing that God's truth will stand no matter what they do. Instead, they are free to be God's witnesses without the pressure of coming to the rescue of truth. In this way, they can spend time listening to God's leading and responding to how he wants them to interact with people in difficult circumstances. In this way, they can love others without the compulsion to *set the record straight*. There is no need to make an immediate choice between truth and relationships.

When there is a conflict, Hiebert described the common response: "Critical realists are willing to continue the dialogue in their common search of the Bible to resolve disputes. If this fails, they maintain relationships despite disagreements because they know that one or both parties may have misunderstood the Biblical texts, and because they are called to love everyone."[3]

Now that we have talked a bit about how Valley Dwellers deal with conflict, let's summarize with Hiebert's words: "Faced with disagreements, positivists attack one another as false, instrumentalists smile and go their own ways . . . and critical realists go back and search the Bible to test their different points of view."[4]

Relating among Truth Lenses

Hopefully, as you have walked through the truth lenses with us, you have a new perspective on what you believe about truth and how that differs from the way other people relate to truth. But there is a lingering question, How am I to relate with someone who doesn't view truth the same way I do?

Maybe you've experienced this type of situation in your own life. It is part of everyday life to come into close contact with people in various stages of their truth lens journey. Though all may look like they come from the same place, one person may be settled on a rock, another ready to jump into the river, while another has lived on the other side for quite some time.

We all like to spend time with people who are like us. Within each truth lens community, there is a sense of mutual understanding of the rules. But with globalization and immigration, spending time with people like us is less and less likely. We constantly find ourselves in situations where people do not see the world the way we do, and we have to decide how to respond—argue, withdraw, or engage.

In disagreements the question of truth lenses rarely is discussed directly. Instead, the issue is the primary focus, and the truth lens is simply the instrument by which the individuals craft their understanding of the issue. This is one reason why when two people with different truth lenses interact, very little progress is made.

We've seen this disconnect play out in different ways in conference rooms, around kitchen tables, and on long road trips. Each person tries to help others understand how he or she views the issue, using various methods to keep the peace or defend a stance. Thinking through this can also help us decide how God wants us to interact with others on questions of truth. Understanding others' truth lenses also helps us think through why people react in many different ways.

In positivist-instrumentalist truth lens interactions, the Rock Dweller does not see the individual aspect of truth discovery and the Island Dweller does not believe it is valid to share truth with others. The result is they talk past each other. In the spirit of *being the bigger person*, the Christian Rock Dweller who is striving to love a neighbor may slip into silent mode on an issue, adopting the tolerant stance to keep the peace. This, however, does not promote growth within the relationship and usually leaves the Rock Dweller feeling as if truth has been betrayed. Most likely, the relationship will not be long term, since either the Rock Dweller will feel the need to defend the truth or the Island Dweller will withdraw. Often the Rock Dweller will only be able to tolerate the Island Dweller's open view for a certain amount of time and will not continue to relate.

In positivist-critical realist truth lens interactions, there may be frustration when the Valley Dweller does not take a solid stand on an issue and leaves the door open to receiving more information. Sometimes Valley Dwellers are accused of fuzzy thinking. The issue is that the rules for learning are different. Valley Dwellers do not necessarily want to debate an issue using powers of logic and persuasion to win the argument. They are open to more subjective approaches to coming to a solution. The logical debate is so engrained in the Rock Dweller's culture that a discussion on a matter without debate feels strange. A game where nobody wins (or everybody does) doesn't seem to have a point. Another stressor in discussions may be in the refusal of Valley Dwellers to acknowledge logic and objective observation as the only way of knowing, though they certainly respect these as important ways of knowing. Rock Dwellers may at first think that Valley Dwellers are starting from the same foundations when they agree together on their respect for reason, but then Rock Dwellers become confused when Valley Dwellers embrace other ways of knowing.

In critical realist-instrumentalist truth lens interactions, it may be difficult to make progress on an issue beyond sharing experiences. Because Valley Dwellers have a need to learn more and discover truth through a community of learners, the relationship may remain superficial, unless the Island Dweller chooses to stay engaged. Then the learning may be one-sided, since the Island Dweller sees truth as personal and is unable or unwilling to participate in the learning. The good thing about this combination is that there is hope for the relationship, since the Island Dweller will most likely not break relationship with the Valley Dweller based on the view of knowable truth, and the Valley Dweller does not see argument as an effective means of change.

Bridging Gaps in Relationships

Thinking about the tools we use to think with, including our truth lenses, is not an easy job. It can be overwhelming. But as you can see, it is important to think about, especially in a world where coworkers in that cluster of cubicles and family members at the birthday party all wear different truth lenses. How can we all live and work together? It is essential that we find truthful, loving ways.

This is also a necessary exercise for people relating cross-generationally. Though truth lenses are not worn exclusively by any one age group, there certainly are trends. Grandparents may see grandchildren going into the river and feel afraid. Grandparents may call to them from the rocky shore, pleading for them to carefully make their way back. When they see their grandchildren bob out of sight, it can be frightening and even bring with it a sense of despair. They believe their loved ones are lost. However, studying River Town with its three truth lenses that have strong holds on our world today should give these grandparents relief and a sense of hope. Their loved ones may not come back to the rocky shore, but there is hope that they may arrive safely on the other side, with a solid foundation of truth and with answers to the nagging questions that sent them swimming in the first place.

But though the seeker can have hope for finding answers and their loved ones can have a sense of relief that they may not be lost forever, is there hope for harmony in relationships between people of different truth lenses?

Because God's worldview is above all cultures and perspectives, we believe the answer is a firm yes. It's not easy; it takes time and understanding. But in a spirit of humility and with God's help, we do have hope to build strong relationships and help each other along the way to knowing God and his world more fully, despite our varied truth lenses.

Resisting Easy Categories

As Hiebert's book demonstrates, this is a complex topic requiring a multidisciplinary approach to understand it thoroughly. We've tried to provide word pictures and analogies that can help to make these concepts as warm and organic as the people who use them everyday. It's very helpful to find a vocabulary that describes something so close to our daily lives. But there is a downfall to putting simple words to something we already know deep down. One downfall is the temptation to look at the characteristics described in each truth lens and begin to label ourselves and those around us: "He is a Rock Dweller because he is so _____." "Oh, now I understand why she is so _____; she is an Island Dweller." But visible actions are not always representative of where people are on their journeys. The words and pictures here create opportunities for discussion that can build bridges of understanding within growing relationships. It is a way to learn together and help each other along the way. Learning about truth lenses may give us the words to talk with others and to prayerfully consider how closely our assumptions are in agreement with how God looks at truth.

Now let's follow a family's truth journey so we can better understand our truth lenses and how we can interact with others in a way that honors God.

Chapter 10

INTERACTING WITH OTHERS ON THE JOURNEY

A s we seek to apply these truth lenses in very practical ways in our lives, one of the most effective ways is to see them in action. Let's walk through some of these issues with a fictional family that deals with the same life struggles that most of us do.

Part I: Stewart and Allison

Stewart and Allison both came from strong Christian homes in the midwestern United States. They met in college at the state university while attending a campus ministry group meeting. They immediately connected on many levels. They enjoyed studying, liked the same music, and were especially interested in growing in their faith and sharing that faith with others. As they spent time together, their love grew. In their third year at the university they got married. It wasn't easy being married and studying, but they felt their relationship was stronger for it.

After they graduated, Stewart got a job as a lab technician and began to work his way up in the company. Through his integrity and competent, precise work, he gained respect and was given increased responsibility. He had a knack for problem solving, and so became the advisor for all difficult setbacks in the lab. Allison worked as a nurse, and enjoyed seeing how her study of biology was helping people get well and return to their daily lives. She had a way of helping people understand how following the doctor's plan would help them recover.

Stewart struggled to integrate his faith with his work. Most of the people in the office did not understand how he could believe in God and at the same time believe in science. He couldn't explain it except that he had a relationship with Jesus that was based on faith, and science was based on science. Most of the time it didn't bother him, but there was the occasional person who would ask him questions that forced him to put the two together. He always felt defensive in those moments.

Allison's struggles came when suffering patients reached out for answers to nagging questions such as, If God is good, why am I in so much pain? These were hard questions coming from real people. She knew the pain was physical, but they needed a spiritual answer. How could she reconcile the pain and suffering and her trust in God?

In the face of the difficulty of sharing their faith with people in their community, the couple held on to their hope of reaching out by supporting several missionaries who were doing evangelism in other countries. They wished they could do more for their neighbors and coworkers, but people just didn't seem to want to hear about God anymore.

As they became more established and bought a home, Ethan came along. All through the pregnancy, Stewart and Allison talked about the things they would like to teach him. Holding him in their arms, they would imagine the kind of man he would grow to be, and they were overwhelmed with love and pride at the blessing God had given them.

Throughout his childhood, Stewart taught Ethan how to tackle problems. Father and son spent many hours in the wood shop behind the house, working on projects and honing their skills. Ethan will never forget the rocking horse project he undertook for his baby cousin. He was having trouble designing the curve of the rocker to fit with the angle of the horse's feet. His dad got out the calculator and the compass, and patiently showed him how to work through the problem, step by step, until it rocked perfectly. That's how Ethan was trained to approach life: see the problem, understand it, pull it apart, design a plan, and put it back together again. It worked so well for so many things that it seemed like a given in life.

Ethan embraced the faith of his parents with all his heart and mind. He loved to memorize verses in church and was always a top qualifier in the Bible challenges. He was bright and absorbed the Bible stories easily and wholeheartedly. He knew the basics of faith through and through and was confident in God and in his salvation.

The family took their love for precision and applied it to their search for a church. They chose a church after studying the written beliefs and after a lengthy breakfast with the pastor during which they dialogued concerning all the hard issues. After seeing that they agreed on most things, they decided they could become active members of the church.

Choosing a college for Ethan was a family event. Allison and Stewart were hoping Ethan would choose a school that would affirm the values they encouraged at home. He chose a small private school several states away. This made Allison happy, since coming home for holidays would not be too difficult. It was during that first visit home for Thanksgiving that Stewart and Allison noticed a change in their son.

The struggle was extra troubling because Ethan's change wasn't an outward one. He didn't change the color or style of his hair or come home with a tattoo. His attitude wasn't rebellious either, but he was asking questions and could not seem to find answers in the foundation his parents had laid for him. It wasn't even the decisions Ethan made that bothered his parents. He still lived and acted with the same morals, but the friends he was making did not follow the same standard. What made things confusing was that this didn't seem to bother Ethan. It was as if the decisions of others did not touch him.

This change was concerning for Stewart and Allison. They worried about his spiritual life, but talking about the issues seemed to push Ethan away. They decided to wait and see . . . and pray that God would give him the answers somehow.

Debriefing Positivism in Action

We can see that Allison and Stewart were brought up in positivism and that their faith is interacting with their truth lens in their family, their church, and their work. In many ways it is an advantage because it gives them security in the certainty of their beliefs, and they are comfortable making decisions based on the pile of truth they have accumulated. This value of objective logic works so well in our modern culture that both Stewart and Allison have been able to be successful in work and in their personal lives.

Overall, their life together is stable, happy, and predictable. But the nagging questions that come up in their individual lives are dealt with by putting these different parts of their lives into silos. They do this because they have no way to make the different areas of life (for example, their work and their faith) compatible.

They approached their search for a church the same way they would approach their job. They sized up the many aspects of the particular congregation along with the theology of the pastor and then made a sensible choice that matched their view of truth. They viewed success in this matter and most other matters as truth alignment.

One of their tendencies has been to ask the *how* questions and overlook or avoid the *why* questions. For example, in the personal relationships at work, Allison would probably focus on how to make a patient feel better emotionally rather than why this patient is struggling.

Whether in their small wood shop, their church, or in their jobs, the couple strives to approach each aspect of their lives fully and with confidence. When they don't feel that confidence, they set out with tenacity to find out why and resolve it.

So when Ethan came home from college with questions and a vocabulary that did not connect with their certainty, they immediately grew alarmed. His college experience had disturbed his way of looking at truth.

This kind of disequilibrium happens often in our world today. It may not be a child coming home from college. It may happen when you connect with an old friend who has changed significantly or when your spouse starts a new job and is spending time with a new set of coworkers.

Part II: Ethan

Ethan was excited to unpack his parent's car and get settled on campus. His roommate seemed fun and spontaneous, and Ethan had the feeling this was going to be an adventure. Bright and energetic, he got involved right away in several activities. He was most excited about the debate team and looked forward to meeting the others in the group.

The debate group was surprisingly varied. Ethan had expected a group of clean-cut guys who had been on debate teams in high school, but what he found was an eclectic group of students interested in discussing issues. In fact, the whole campus reflected more variety than Ethan had ever experienced. People from other countries, backgrounds, and experiences surrounded him. He began to build close friendships and spend late nights talking about life with these new people. He was surprised to discover so many different perspectives. At the same time, his classes were presenting information that challenged some of his beliefs, and this bothered him.

He decided to tackle the new questions the way his dad taught him to in the wood shop. He did this through the debate team.

Every problem he faced he pulled apart, developed an argument, and presented his case. He was good at it, but the opponents on his team were also good. They developed arguments as sound as his, and again he was disturbed. How could two people using the same tools of logic and reason come up with such different answers? Shouldn't they agree? Many hours were spent presenting sides and discussing strategy, but that core question never resolved: If I can't know something for certain through logic, what can I know for sure? The thought nagged at him. These were the questions he brought home with him that Thanksgiving of his freshman year.

Over time he began to conclude that the answers must be different for everyone and that agreeing was futile and unnecessary. He still believed in God and knew that he could work in his life, but it changed how he felt about sharing his faith. His beliefs became more personal, and he became tolerant of other beliefs, not feeling as though he had a right to question what others believed. This came in very handy when it came to living with his roommate. Likable and fun, the roommate didn't worry about decisions very much. He did whatever he felt was okay and lived everyday like it was his last. When he brought girls into the room, Ethan just excused himself politely and found somewhere else to study. When he pushed the rules, Ethan looked the other way. What right did Ethan have to say anything?

For the next four years on summer break and Christmas vacations, Ethan brought home many questions. He stopped bringing his friends because he saw how difficult it was for his parents. Little by little it began to be harder and harder for him to be home, too. His parents always seemed to be fighting the evil in the world, and he shied away from the debate. He often felt the need to defuse the judgment he felt they were making on people and their beliefs.

Ethan continued to think this way through graduation. His first job was with a temp agency. Having a degree in business administration, he tried to learn how to make good hiring decisions by working with all kinds of people. Ethan was impressed by his boss, Stephen, who encouraged a team spirit and invested time with all the employees, not just seeing them as objects to fill open slots. Ethan realized that he could learn from him.

During Ethan's first month on the job his roommate walked into the agency with a big smile. After talking a little about the summer and what had been going on in their lives, the roommate asked if he could fill out an application. Ethan gave him one that he filled out quickly and returned to Ethan. When he left, Ethan looked over the application and noticed that to the question, Have you ever taken illegal drugs? the roommate had checked no. Hmm. Ethan knew for certain that this was not true, and a sudden pain shot through him. What should he do? When it didn't concern him, Ethan was happy to turn the other way; but this untruth conflicted with his responsibility to the agency. Ethan put the application into the file drawer and took a coffee break to think through what he should do. He decided to put it on Stephen's desk with a suggestion for a job placement.

A few days later a company called Stephen, angry that the roommate had not come. Ethan felt awful. He had known the character of his roommate, and against his better judgment, still recommended placing him in a job. Ethan's actions had adversely affected others. A couple weeks later, Stephen called Ethan into his office. It was his ninety-day review, and Ethan was interested in not only the input he would get but also observing how Stephen conducted the meeting.

Stephen demonstrated his same style of teamwork and open communication. In the meeting they discussed the roommate situation. Instead of arguing, the two men were able to talk about Ethan's dilemma and why he didn't know what the right decision was. Stephen suggested that they continue talking about this over coffee on Thursday mornings before work. And so began their weekly meetings.

In the meetings the two of them talked about many of the nagging questions Ethan had struggled with over the years. Stephen had thought-provoking comments to make, and Ethan began to understand that there may be a way to accept other people while still holding onto firm beliefs and values. Faith began to make more sense to Ethan once Stephen explained that it was not necessary to make the discovery of truth completely logical or completely personal. It was exciting to think that it was possible to learn from others through close relationships, rather than just live side by side in peace.

Debriefing Instrumentalism in Action

Ethan went to college very confident in what he knew—so much so that he joined the debate team. But soon he became exposed to many other perspectives on the world, and he realized that these new perspectives could not be so easily dismissed. He was exposed to many new ideas, and he was not ready to handle all this new information. He was caught off guard by obvious flaws in objective thinking that he had never wrestled with and started to accept the personal nature of knowledge as more reliable than the objective arguments his parents had taught him.

This was very practical when living in his new environment. He was able to have friendships with many different kinds of people, without the dissonance he would have felt before. The first great disturbance he faced came when he tried to relate to his parents on his first visit home. He had to reject his parents' assumptions as Rock Dwellers for his new identity as an Island Dweller to stay intact. At the same time, his parents didn't see the value of his personal perspective and his broader acceptance of new ideas and people. Ethan and his parents were talking but not connecting because they did not respect or value each other's view of truth.

One of the greatest challenges for relationships between people using the positivist truth lens and people using the instrumentalist truth lens is that the first lens rejects personal perspective while the second lens rejects absolute, knowable truth. In this way, people using these truth lenses will strive to communicate with each other without realizing that they cannot possibly connect.

The second great disturbance came when he ignored his roommate's lie on the application form. Up to this point, the instrumentalist truth lens had served Ethan as a "useful fiction" that allowed him to get along with everyone and still accomplish what he needed to do at school. But his tolerance of another person's lie had impacted his job, and this caused Ethan a second disturbance. He realized that truth has to make sense in community because the consequences are not just individual—they affect many other people.

Part III: Stephen

During Ethan's job interview, Stephen immediately saw something of himself in this bright, young mind. Sharp, articulate, and caring, Ethan exhibited the qualities Stephen needed in someone who would help him build a staff of dependable temp workers. He loved working with people and watching them mature. He saw people as amazing creations, capable of growth and change.

When the roommate situation unfolded, Stephen was disappointed and yet not surprised. He could see that Ethan's caring attitude wanted to give everyone a chance. He obviously had a faith in God that he was personally committed to, but this faith wasn't working out in his job as might be expected. He wanted to help Ethan grow through this conflict so he could improve in his discernment skills that would be critical as he worked with people.

Ethan candidly asked Stephen, "How can I judge character without infringing on personal beliefs and choices?" Stephen answered, "Don't you think that their ideas of truth affect all of us? Truth affects the whole community, not just one person. What was the impact of your roommate's ethics on you, your job, this company, and our reputation?"

Stephen was in his element. Coffee meetings like these with employees he mentored were what Stephen lived for. It was exciting to help people learn, grow, and develop their skills. He could see that Ethan and the other employees were not only becoming more competent, but they were also more connected with each other and to people at the companies who used their services. This was what made Stephen truly happy in his job.

One particular Thursday morning while Stephen was waiting for Ethan at their regular table, he reflected on his own journey. It was true; there were many parts of his life that weren't as exciting as those mentoring hours. Stephen felt as if he lived in a world where few people understood him. There were many people who saw him as fuzzy, wishy-washy, and unable to take a hard stand or answer questions directly. Many encouraged him to take a tough love approach to the people on his team, but he resisted, believing that developing a truth lens is a process that takes time and patience.

Part of the problem was the language he lived with. So many either/or statements excluded the possibility of finding a solution that incorporated the bigger picture. It made his language sound less certain than he actually felt. It was true that he was comfortable with questions that don't have immediate answers, but he had come to terms with the unknown without it necessarily meaning uncertainty. This had allowed for an even stronger faith that fit better into his daily thinking.

As these thoughts swirled in Stephen's head, Ethan's coffee mug banged down on their small round table and grabbed his attention. He shook off his thoughts and focused on the young man in front of him. Ethan had seemed anxious to talk all week—ever since he returned on Monday from his parents' house. Last Thursday Ethan had shared how nervous he was about going home. After many negative visits, he was certain that something would torpedo the event and leave his relationship with them a little more strained than it already was.

But as Stephen watched the young man take his first sip of coffee, he knew it had gone well. Ethan told the highlights of his weekend. "It only took two hours for some of the same old issues to crop up," he said. But the conversation had not taken its usual turn. Ethan explained how he had taken Stephen's advice from the Thursday before. Instead of retreating when his parents pressed him for absolutes, he engaged with them and took a learning stance.

The first issue to come up had been his job. Ethan had told his parents how much he loved the job and the process of helping people find a good job fit. His dad jumped in right away and wanted to know all about how the hiring process was structured. He drilled him on the computer testing, the points system, and the final tally. Ethan happily relayed all the details, but as soon as Ethan began explaining about the intuitive side of placing a person, his dad's attitude changed; those same resistant walls went up.

For the first time Ethan saw what was causing his dad to be frustrated with him. He explained to Stephen how he was able to respond. Ethan described the foundation of testing and then explained that there were holes in using testing alone to place a person in a job. When his dad rejected that idea offhand, Ethan asked him if he could relate some stories of specific people.

His dad grudgingly agreed and then became more and more interested as Ethan's stories unfolded. Ethan told his dad about the importance of learning about people and what they value. He also explained how he had been involved in the same process of learning. As his mom listened, she got engaged in the discussion and began talking about how, even though she had a base plan of care from her doctor for a particular patient, knowing the patient personally was helpful in understanding the whole person and how to truly care for them.

Ethan then told Stephen how his dad had jumped in, encouraged by his mom's example, and had begun to ask questions about how Ethan was combining the hard test data with the soft personal perspective on a person in making evaluations for hiring.

And so the evening had gone. Ethan recounted how his parents had slowly realized that he had not lost his faith or his belief in truth, but that he was learning that coming to a full understanding of truth is a process.

Stephen smiled at the story and knew that Ethan's journey through the river was almost over.

Debrief of Critical Realism in Action

Stephen's approach is an example of relating to others as a Valley Dweller. He started out with the basic understanding that Ethan's ignoring his roommate's lying on the application was wrong, but he also saw and affirmed the motivation behind Ethan's decision. Instead of jumping on Ethan for an infraction, Stephen saw it as a learning opportunity for him. Stephen did not back away from confronting the issue, because he had a foundation of right and wrong on which to stand. However, the truth he was standing on was not his only concern. He wanted Ethan to think through why he made certain decisions so he could make better decisions in the future. He wanted Ethan to grow.

The weekly coffee sessions are a great example of the learning approach. Stephen saw that he could pass on the value of asking *why* before asking *how*. He wanted Ethan to begin to connect the dots among the different ways of knowing about the world around him.

Understanding this learning approach allowed Ethan to bridge the divide between him and his parents. He was able to validate his parent's desire for knowable truth, because he did see the value in things that were knowable and certain. However, he used what he objectively knew as a platform to introduce other ways of knowing that made his job more successful and gave him a fuller understanding of those he was trying to help.

In the end, Ethan helped his parents by introducing them to ways they could integrate what they believed in their daily life. He gave them much to think about. It also helped Ethan think about how to begin relating to God a little differently. He realized that God was bigger than his understanding of him. God was no longer someone to figure out, nor was he someone who was only personal to him. God could be known as he revealed himself to people. God was also someone he could feel comfortable sharing with others, knowing that the truth of God is both personal and universal.

Bringing It All Together

As you can see from this story, although truth lenses are invisible to us, they affect our lives and relationships deeply. Each day we interact with people from every different truth lens. Many times we wonder why it is easy to build a relationship with one person, but very difficult with another person.

Some of our challenges in communication and conflict were exemplified as Ethan and his parents interacted, as Ethan and his roommate related, and as Ethan engaged with his boss. This simple story about Ethan and his relationships can be mirrored in each of our lives in countless ways. Many times we can see that there is a problem with our relationships, but we can't find the source of the issues. How we view truth is often that source, and by thinking about what we think with, we can make progress toward understanding and growth in our relationships.

The Next Step

Once we understand our personal journeys and relationships, we are ready to look beyond our immediate surroundings. This new understanding will provide us with an entirely new way of sharing truth with those around us. As we move into the next chapter, we will focus on how our truth lenses impact our outreach in our communities, our country, and the wider world.

Chapter 11

THE WORLD THROUGH YOUR TRUTH LENS

I n River Town there are more differences among the residents than just their truth lenses. Some of the residents are Christians and others are not. The Christians in each community gather together in churches and enjoy each other's company within strong relationships. One aspect of church ministry is programs and strategies to reach out to those in their community and beyond their borders in the hope of seeing unbelievers come to faith as well as seeing believers grow in their relationship with God.

The thinking about outreach looks very different depending on whether you are attending church on the rocky shore, the sandy islands, or in the valley on the far shore. These different approaches bring both positive and negative results to the surrounding communities. As you read the next pages, you will be exposed to Hiebert's thinking on how truth lenses impact missions. These ideas came from his years of experience, and we believe they can be easily applied to local outreach and global ministry.

The World from the Rocky Shore

Because the rocky shore was settled first, the initial patterns of outreach were established by the Rock Dwellers. The message was logically laid out to take the stories of the Bible and frame them around the key truths that everyone needs to know. Rock Dwellers didn't think much about differences in culture. While they brought their culture with them, their main objective was to present the truth completely and clearly.

This is because they "defined the gospel largely in terms of knowledge."[1] This meant that they acted much like lawyers in a courtroom. The goal of outreach for a Rock Dweller is to present and defend the truth so that (with the help of logic and factual information) another person would come to salvation.

As Hiebert compared positivism to a legal role, he cited E. Stanley Jones.[2] This idea is important because it colors everything about how a Rock Dweller approaches outreach and ministry. As a lawyer pleads to a jury the merits of a case, so Rock Dwellers see their job as laying out the reasons why the gospel is the true path for others to adopt. The phrase that best describes what they have in mind is "winning the lost to Christ," just as a lawyer would desire to win a case for a client.

One of the prominent places in the Bible that speaks about outreach in this way is 1 Corinthians 9:19-23. In this passage Paul talked about what it takes to win the lost for Christ. Paul's emphatic presentation shows his heart of sacrifice and his passion to see the lost redeemed. This resonates with a Rock Dweller because it is goal oriented and can show specific progress toward a person's fuller understanding of the truth.

On the rocky shore there is a strong tendency to see the world as separated between body and soul. Rock Dwellers will focus on the work of evangelism separate from their work in mercy ministries. Many times they will use the mercy ministries to gain entrée into the lives of those they are seeking to reach. The challenge with this is that many times people accept the mercy but do not go on to accept the truth that is presented. This truth lens does not see value in equal integration of mercy and proclamation; instead, it puts priority on the sharing of truth. When talking about nineteenth- and twentieth-century missions, Hiebert put it this way, "It also led many missionaries to see their task as twofold; as evangelism and church planting to Christianize the people, and as building schools and hospitals to civilize them. The latter were often seen as tools to achieve the former."[3]

When Rock Dwellers are reaching out beyond their culture or religion, one of their main desires is to see those who embrace the truth abandon much of their culture and religion. Rock Dwellers tend to see anything from outside of the message as potentially harmful to it. So Rock Dwellers want new Christians to replace many cultural practices with ones that are more aligned with their own cultures and Christianity as they have experienced it.

Hiebert gave an example from India that helps explain this clearly. "Moreover, because in most societies all areas of life have religious significance, few local symbols and customs could be used in the church. For example, in India it was the custom for Hindu women to use red saris at their weddings to symbolize fertility.

Many missionaries rejected red because it was used by Hindus and substituted white, even though in India white symbolized barrenness and death . . . the result was a confrontational approach to other religions."[4]

The World from the Islands

As people left the rocky shore for the islands, their truth lens affected how they reached out to share their faith. They reacted to the strong message that pointed to only one way of viewing truth. Instead, outreach shifted from delivering truth to delivering love through dialogue. Outreach began to focus on felt needs rather than eternal destiny. Those reaching out became less and less driven by spiritual growth and more focused on improving the world around them.

This focus on physical needs sprang out of seeing their faith as very personal and truth as nontransferable. Believing in Christ did not always immediately change a person's truth lens, and a person could come into relationship with Jesus and still retain certain incorrect assumptions about truth. Left in instrumentalism, a person's faith focused on felt needs and their Christianity became extremely personal. This focus on felt needs is everywhere in our culture because people are trying to take very personal needs and forge some commonality through dialogue.

This dialogue came out of the strong belief that only experience is real. Hiebert explained, "The goal in missions, in an instrumentalist epistemology, is dialogue—to attempt to understand and learn from those in other religions and to find some grounds for agreement. It is not to lead people to faith in Jesus Christ as the only way to salvation."[5]

Dialogue helps a person affirm others, but then leaves them to face their journeys alone. This means that outreach starts with the physical needs of a person and from there focuses on listening and understanding the other person's spiritual journey. Island Dwellers are not listening to decide whether other people should change their beliefs or get help in understanding truth. Instead, they listen as a sign of respect to all beliefs as valid approaches in people's search for God.

Everyone's search for God is seen as valid as this truth lens focuses on championing dignity and freedom. Instrumentalism leads us away from thinking about eternity and focuses on present needs. This makes causes such as democracy and human rights in far away lands very attractive to Island Dwellers. They want others to have the same freedom to define their own realities.

Because instrumentalism is knowledge personally defined, felt needs are a critical element of outreach. Hiebert said, "Mission is also ministry to people according to their felt needs. We must begin where people are and let them define the agenda and the solutions. We must focus on this world and the present."[6] Outreach focused on felt needs looks more like humanitarian aid, education, and economic programs than evangelism. All these things meet the felt needs of others without having to deal with their personal views about truth (which cannot be challenged and should not be changed).

The challenge with outreach in the river is that it becomes very shallow. The instrumentalist outreach of the Island Dweller is a reaction to the drawbacks found on the rocky shore of positivism. But instead of bridging the gap between natural and supernatural needs, it focuses almost exclusively on the natural needs because the supernatural ones are seen as nontransferable. Instead of providing eternal solutions, it works to ease pain and suffering and give opportunity to those who need it. There is nothing wrong with this in and of itself; however, it is not an answer to the questions that Jesus addressed as he walked the land of Israel so many years ago. Hiebert warned, "Ultimately, instrumentalism leads us to religious relativism and to the denial of the uniqueness of Christ as the only way of salvation."[7]

The World from the Far Shore

When some of the people reached the far shore, their new perspective gave them a different approach to reaching out to unbelievers. They realized that truth was an essential element of the message that they could boldly share with others, while also admitting the importance of personal experience and perspective. Their outreach efforts focused on the person they were reaching out to, taking into consideration each individual journey. Their approach was enriched by the love they had identified on the islands, while holding onto a strong faith they fostered on the rocky shore.

One of the most unique characteristics of the outreach from this truth lens is the ability to hold to foundational truth while working within the world of human ambiguity. This means that a person can bear witness to things that they know about God, and do it in a way that allows them to learn from those they are sharing with. "Critical realists hold to objective truth but recognize that it is understood by humans in their contexts. There is, therefore, an element of faith and personal commitment in the knowledge of truth."⁸ When those using the critical realist truth lens look at opportunities for outreach, they strive to help people understand the message and begin to apply it to their daily lives. A verse that resonates with Valley Dwellers as they seek to share the gospel is Ephesians 4:15: "But speaking the truth in love, we must grow up in every way into him who is the head, into Christ" (NRSV).

This approach requires love, humility, and patience to see the Holy Spirit working within the lives of the people they are reaching out to. E. Stanley Jones said, "When I was called to the ministry, I had a vague notion that I was to be God's lawyer: I was to argue his case for him and put it up brilliantly . . . I got the lesson never to be forgotten: in my ministry I was to be, not God's lawyer, but his witness." Hiebert added that critical realists "are not interested in winning an argument but in winning the lost for Christ."⁹

In the past, people reaching out to others were more likely to see themselves as lawyers with the responsibility of persuading other people to see truth the way they saw it. The approach, though it had a component of faith, was more focused on head knowledge than it was on relationship. In critical realism the focus shifts toward helping others understand the message in the context of their lives. This means that people reaching out may begin with a need in a person's life and then apply the truth to it.

An example of this is outreach by showing a popular movie. The person showing the movie starts with something that is part of a person's context and shows how God's truth applies to this experience. Or perhaps people are struggling with a relationship in their lives and don't know how to approach it. Valley Dwellers have the ability to begin with people's questions and lead them into truth from there. One of the big differences is that when Rock Dwellers are working with individuals who disagree with them, they see the challenge as one of acceptance or rejection. Valley Dwellers see interactions as opportunities for learning, rather than opportunities for persuasion.

So how do Valley Dwellers stay faithful to the foundation of truth as they continue learning through life? It begins with the recognition that "the Holy Spirit is at work in the lives of young believers, guiding them in their understanding of the truth."[10] This takes the control out of the hands of the one sharing and puts it with God, where it belongs. As witnesses, we can walk with others through their questions, praying that God will give them understanding of his truth in their lives. The responsibility for persuading remains with God.

The learning approach is effective because one approach for every culture cannot succeed: people in different cultures and situations ask different questions. God may bring understanding to a certain culture in different areas than another culture. This is exciting because as the world becomes more connected, we can learn together the insights God is revealing to us and all gain a fuller understanding of the truth. Because God is the author of truth, what we share should be complementary, not contradictory. If as we learn together we discover a contradiction, this is an opportunity to continue to look for resolution. The key here is that we have not given up on the fact that there is truth in the situation; we just realize that it is a truth we are learning. This approach takes the control out of our hands and puts it into God's.

Outreach through learning will only happen if the church and Christians worldwide will commit to learning together and sharing what they learn. As we saw in instrumentalism, dialogue became the replacement for the confrontation of positivist outreach. In critical realism, dialogue takes on a whole new dimension. "Here dialogue helps us to build understanding and trust with non-Christians, to find bridges of communication with them, and to help us discriminate between truth and error in their beliefs. It can also challenge us to reexamine our own understandings of and commitment to our biblical faith."[11]

Like Island Dwellers, the Valley Dwellers see value in meeting felt needs. But simply meeting these needs is not sufficient, nor do they see it as a means to an end. The Valley Dweller approaches felt needs as part of a process of learning God's truth. "Today we realize that we must bring a whole gospel. . . . We may need to start with felt needs, but we must move to the ultimate human needs of salvation, reconciliation, justice, and peace, both here and in eternity."[12]

Daily Outreach

Let's imagine that you are standing with a group of people from your office and your heart sinks when Ben says, "So what did you think about the debate last night?" These kinds of conversations were never good. Conversations with Ben always made people silent or angry, and always uncomfortable. You throw a half-smile at Christy next to you and look down at your scuffed shoes. Christy is a sweet girl in the marketing department. You recently had lunch with her several times and had the opportunity to share Jesus with her. On several occasions, she had said how Ben was hard to be around because he was always trying to get her to agree with him and wouldn't just accept her beliefs and move on.

You cringe as Ben tries to engage Christy in the conversation. Everyone knows that you and Ben go to church together, so you feel that Ben's actions reflect on you. Sure, you like Ben. He has strong opinions about many things and can talk about them informatively. Recently, he gave a knowledgeable talk on Noah and the flood in your Sunday school class, and you enjoyed his point-by-point presentation. He has a great mind for detail and is an excellent researcher.

But Christy isn't a fighter. She stays to herself mostly, and when asked about difficult things, she simply says that it is a personal matter to her. How could you share the truth of Jesus with Christy when Ben is always framing truth in such a definitive way? When Ben says to you, "You agree with me, don't you?" what do you say? You basically agree with Ben's conclusion, but not for the same reasons, and not how he talks about it.

You decide that you will e-mail Christy and ask if she is free for lunch today. When you get the message that she is, you pray that God will give you wisdom to know what to say to her. As you walk together to the bagel shop on the corner, you start by asking her how her mother is. You know that her health has been declining, and so you are genuinely concerned. Christy says that her mother doesn't really have much time left and that it is hard to think about. She asks, "What am I going to do without her? What does it all mean?"

You immediately empathize. You say, "I remember when my grandmother passed away and God really taught me some things through the process. Could I show you the scrapbook I made about her and some of the lessons I found along the way?" Christy is thankful for the opportunity and she agrees to go shopping on Saturday and have lunch at your house to continue the conversation. Through the process Christy asks many questions about grief, dying, and what it all means. You are able to walk through the Bible verses that touched your life, and you can see that she is beginning to see how your God and faith in him applies to her life and situation very specifically. You pray that this journey of questions and learning will bring her into relationship with Jesus.

Daily Outcomes

In this little story we tried to depict how the different truth lenses will approach and interact in an outreach situation. Many different variables play out in our daily lives as people of different faiths and truth lenses meet. In our story we showed how the Rock Dweller struggled to connect with the Island Dweller, because they did not value the same aspects of truth. The Valley Dweller's approach of process and learning connected with both the Island Dweller's search for answers to the deeper questions of life and also with the Rock Dweller's value of knowable truth. So, the Valley Dweller's approach bridged a gap by valuing personal perspective as well as objective truth.

The most important realization is that your truth lens will affect the way you interact with others in sharing your faith. Think about the people you are trying to interact with, while you are reading this book. What do they respond to? What truth lens are they using? Based on what you've learned in this book about truth lenses, how does this help you to respond to the needs of others and connect with them?

Your understanding of your truth lens will give you great insight into how you approach reaching out to others and may help you connect with the people God puts on your heart.

Encouraging Your Heart

It is always helpful to hear about the journeys of others. There is so much to learn about truth lenses and how they impact our daily decisions. But this can become intellectual and difficult to put into practice, so in the final chapter we would like to share Dr. Hiebert's story as well as our own. We hope that this will be a great encouragement as you seek to understand your own truth lens on your journey.

Chapter 12

JOURNEYS THROUGH THE RIVER

In his own journey across the river, Dr. Hiebert described the Valley Dweller's critical realist approach to truth as "a way ahead."[1] One of the practical results of critical realism that makes this a good description is that the assumptions and resulting thought patterns pull us back to God when we slip into trusting ourselves and our own strength. A critical realist truth lens will remind us that we can't know everything fully, but that there is someone who does, and we must depend on him to guide us to all truth.

Critical realism says things like, "We are finite; there is hope to know more; we can learn together." Questions and conflicts between faith and reason do not have to raise doubts and fears that my whole structure of knowledge is going to crumble, but they provide a challenge to keep searching for an integrated solution, if we hold onto faith and learn together.

In this world where so many conflicts are the result of what Hiebert called the "clash of epistemologies," there are many people beginning their journey across the river.[2] Holding onto their beliefs in a knowable world, these travelers long for a better way that will allow them to love others without giving up truth. They want to know and be known, and they feel this great disturbance deep down. Then, in a moment of faith, they wade out into the water.

At first the river of instrumentalism is scary, and the temptation to turn back is strong. The travelers' families call for them to return, out of fear of losing them to the current. But the disturbance is calling too, without a solution. They keep swimming. They swim because they have a hope of firm ground on the other side. They swim because they have faith in a God that is bigger than their questions. They hope that the same God that asks us to love others has provided a way of knowing truth that will make that possible.

The next question that normally comes to the modern mind is, Now what? Once we see an idea we like, our drive toward progress propels us into action, and we want to do something. We want the one-two-three formula for success in our endeavors. But each of our journeys will be unique. There are no magic formulas for the surprises God may have for us as we seek him in relationship and, in so doing, discover truth.

We want to share our stories with you as you reflect on what we've described. Maybe you are considering whether you will wade into the water. Perhaps you are reflecting on your personal journey, using the concepts and imagery we've provided. You may be thinking about loved ones who have come across the water, and now you have a framework with which to understand what you witnessed in their lives.

Here, we offer our stories, our journeys, and some practical ideas that may be helpful along the way.

Dr. Hiebert's Journey

Our journeys are tied closely to our background and experiences. Dr. Hiebert described himself as an evangelical with Anabaptist roots and as an anthropologist. Growing up in India as part of a missionary family, crosscultural experiences, considerations, and questions were close to his heart. His journey, therefore, began with a disturbance that was a conflict between his truth lens and his work in anthropology and missions. When he realized that his disturbance had its roots in his truth lens, he knew he needed a new tool in order to harmonize theology and anthropology. Instrumentalism was a clear option, but did not offer an acceptable solution with its relativism. So, what was next? He described his discovery this way, "It was then that I discovered the critical approach to realism advocated by Charles Pierce, Ian Barbour, and others. This avoided the arrogance and colonialism implicit in positivism and the relativism of instrumentalism. I found that it fit closely with the teachings of Jesus, Paul and the other New Testament writers. It also made theology a living reality in my life, touching every area of my thought life."[3]

Mindy's Journey

I remember my journey through the river, though at the time I didn't understand that it partly had to do with my truth lens. I knew it had to do with truth and knowing. I knew it had to do with faith. But it was a lonely journey, and it took more than ten years for me to find that there were others who had come out of the river. Traveling through the river was the scariest thing to do. I felt that everything in my life was changing around me, and I could do very little about it except go through the process.

It was early in my college years. Fresh out of a protected childhood and adolescence, I was educated strongly in the dualistic nature of the world and the importance of truth and defending it. My time in secular education was always an exercise in standing for the truth, usually with a little bit of fear and pride.

The class was "Critical Thinking" and the professor preferred to meet in the hallway, on a group of tattered hassocks in the corner. He stood tall and lean, with wavy grey hair falling around a chiseled face that made me think he was in the direct blood line of Aristotle. A wall-sized picture window looked out onto the sunny courtyard where students walked back and forth, laden with books. Using the window as a white board, he scrawled the principles of logic and argument like graffiti across the midwestern sky.

I began the class in a defensive stance, hands balled into fists, knees bent, ready to strike if attacked. I had had many teachers challenge my Christianity in the past, and I instinctively got ready. The professor introduced the class by saying that what we were going to cover wasn't anything new for us. It was all stuff we knew; we just might not know that we knew it. That was unthreatening enough.

For weeks he talked about how we discover truth, how we defend our positions, and how logic works. Over time, I began to realize that as much as I didn't like to admit it, I could not prove through logic that what I believed was true. It was a startling realization. After years of believing that the Christian position could be proven through science and logic, I realized that I couldn't make it work.

For a while, I lived in a lost haze of despair. My former world of security had fallen away, and now, if truth was the sum total of what humans could comprehend through logic, what point was there? I felt darkness closing in.

Yet, there was Jesus and the relationship we had had since I was small. I could not deny those years of intimate experiences: how he had held me up through the death of my Sunday school teacher, how he had been there for every frightening test I had taken, and how I felt his love during the singing on Sunday mornings. I could not deny his leading in the difficult decisions of what school to attend or what I should do in difficult relationships. He had always been there. Logic could not take that away.

And so I was back in class again, looking down the dingy hallway and pondering all of this when I realized that logic may help us discover some truth, but that does not mean it is the only way to discover truth! With that realization, the light of faith shot back into my life. Faith was not based solely on logic and reason, or even my ability to understand. Faith is based on the person of Jesus Christ.

I realize now that I was never alone on my journey. Jesus was right there through the whole thing. When I was swimming through the river and could not feel the bottom, he was swimming next to me. When I was tangled in the reeds and felt like I would surely drown, he watched carefully to make sure I escaped safely. He welcomed me when I came to the shore—wet, tired, and scared.

My truth lens had changed, and the world looked completely different; but he was the same, lovingly holding my hand the entire time.

Most of the closest people in my life noticed that I was going through something, but they didn't know what it was. In many ways, I felt alone, but without the words to communicate the journey I was on. When I crawled out of the river, I was relieved to be on solid ground. Unfortunately, there was no one there to meet me who had gone through a similar experience.

How I wish I had found people on the other shore who could relate! But God is faithful, and years later, he brought into my life a little book with a big title that talked about my journey. Here there were other people who believed it was okay to see through a glass darkly. How thankful I am for the work of Dr. Hiebert, who worked to help Christians see a way past the arguments of positivism and the hopelessness of instrumentalism to find a better way to interact with other cultures. I was thankful for the vocabulary to describe my new view of truth, even ten years later.

A few years ago I was talking with a close family friend in my mom's kitchen. Struggling to find the words to describe what she was feeling, in a spirit of love and caring, she said something like, "When you were really questioning in college, we were worried about you. But now, it seems like you are in a good place, on solid ground." It feels good to be on solid ground that isn't based on reason or my own understanding, but on faith in an infinite God. As I become more comfortable in God's infiniteness, I am more comfortable in my finiteness, with a desire to know more of the One who created me and this world.

Jon's Journey

My life truly has been a journey through this river. Born in Denver, Colorado, when my parents were studying at Denver Seminary, I soon was jetting south to spend time with our Costa Rican nurse while my parents went to language school. From there it was off to northwest Argentina for the rest of my young life. Amazingly, while in Argentina, we lived in the jungle, the country, and in a bustling city . . . each with its own wonders and lessons.

I remember my parents spending hours in a dusty little jungle church while my brother and I played out in the mud. The church was made out of simple wooden planks and we could see through the cracks. I remember their loving service to the Guarani Indians, working the sugar cane fields and discovering this new God and his great love for them.

I look back fondly to the country home where we lived at the foothills of the Andes. We could see the snow frosted mountains in the distance and enjoyed the beauty of the seasons—even if they were opposite of the northern hemisphere. I remember the fan blowing the tinsel on the Christmas tree and playing inside on cold July days. I saw my parents struggle to launch their new ministry and work long hours to build the leadership development program for almost one hundred small churches in the area.

Then came my favorite home. We lived in a nice apartment in the capital of the province—Salta. Our apartment was in front of the largest park in town and within walking distance of my parent's office, the post office, and all of the amenities in the city. My brother and I were older, and we were able to discover and play around the city in a way that would not be possible in a U. S.

city today. I spent many hours collating and folding papers for my parent's extension seminary lessons. I saw the program they had struggled to start explode and grow beyond anything they had thought was possible.

So as Mindy and I began our own ministry after college, I took those lessons and experiences from my parents and began to apply them. But what I had not seen in my parent's work was the amount of ownership and development from the Argentine Christians who worked with them. Of course I was just a kid and didn't pay attention to those sorts of things.

As we launched into our work developing evangelistic websites for youth in various countries and languages, I thought that I was bringing all the answers. I felt that my perspective and my ideas would make my work successful. I assumed that all people looked at their faith the same way I did, and so I approached my work with that perspective.

But as we expanded our online sites and began to hire staff around the world to help us, I realized that online evangelism wasn't going to look the same everywhere. In fact, as I traveled around the world setting up the follow-up and the strategic partnerships, I realized that each language and each culture needed a different experience.

This was solidified as I moved into my next role of running a small technology consultancy focused on helping faith-based nonprofits with innovation projects. I began using designers, developers, and strategists from Ukraine, India, Mexico, and other countries. As I worked with them, I realized that what they brought to the project was so different. They had different ways of processing the issues, and they came up with different solutions.

In many ways I didn't know what to do with this information. I wanted there to be one simple answer to a given problem, and I pushed hard to get it. I was still on the rocky shore of the river, struggling to build up my pile of truth. But I was discovering that the world's complexity hindered me. I found myself frustrated and unable to pull together all of the expectations and values of my clients and vendors.

I didn't find solutions in the quagmire of constant airplane trips, client meetings, and project deadlines. In fact, I found myself constantly frustrated because each culture brought a new reality, and I could not make them all fit together. It was like a puzzle I could not finish. Each time I thought I had an answer for how to manage the projects in these diverse environments, a new twist would appear and I would lose control again. My first great disturbance came out of this confusion. I put my feet in the water and then waded in. I stopped caring about whether I would ever find the answer, and my life was filled with pragmatic goals focused on the success of my little company.

My struggles exploded when it all fell apart. I unexpectedly had to close up shop, and, in that moment, I was left with nothing. I had been managing all of these different expectations, values, and ideals for so long that when it ended I didn't even know what to think. I didn't want to admit that my frustrations with the cultural diversity and the project expectations had brought the investment of my last three years to a quick end.

The failure that I felt impacted me more than I let on. This was my second great disturbance. I knew that I valued working crossculturally and helping nonprofits communicate their messages, but I felt lost in the whirlpool of ideas and thoughts.

None of them seemed to fit together, and everyone seemed to be doing their own thing. I was discouraged by the difficulties of partnerships between organizations. The challenges seemed insurmountable.

After months of wrapping up projects and interviewing for new jobs, a former client—HCJB Global—asked me to be their communications director. I was happy for stability and a focused task to work on. The security of a job within a larger organization allowed me to process my conflicts and struggles that had matured while serving as a consultant. It was in this time that I crossed the river and pulled myself up on the opposite shore. I began to see the world differently. I saw the same problems between cultures in my new job. But there was a difference. I began to see how some basic principles could be interpreted and carried out very differently with success. I watched people share the gospel in very different ways through media and healthcare, while following some basic principles about ministry. It was in this environment and while studying to write this book that I really began to enjoy the idea of "the truth we know and the truth we are learning."

I'm still drying off from my short time in the river. Others stay there longer than I. My greatest challenge as I adapt to the far shore of the river is my many years on the rocky shore. All my schooling and my first years working were defined by positivism. I learned a lot from it, but now as I try to accept a wider under-standing of truth, I look back across the river longingly. There are moments of uncertainty when I long for my mound on which I sat so comfortably before. But at those moments I look around at the friends that I am learning with and I smile at what may happen today as I prepare my heart to learn.

Conclusion

Each of our journeys will be as unique and individual as God created each of us to be. Some will jump in and swim hard. Others will spend more time getting across. Some may put their toes in the cold water and pull them out quickly again.

The journey can be frightening, exciting, even exhilarating. The people in our lives may be cheering us on from one shore and others may be calling us back to what we left. We may be tempted to stay in the river and allow it to pull us downstream. Some people may not even notice that we've left on a journey at all.

The journey is one of faith—faith in the One who is bigger than our questions and who has provided a way to live and love the way he asks us to live and love in the Bible. We are here as an encouragement that there is something beyond the shore of positivism with its promises of certainty; there is more beyond the river of instrumentalism with its promises of peace; there is a shore beyond where critical realism offers a way ahead that offers hope in a knowable world and knowable relationships with others. Your challenge now is to pray, read the Bible, have faith, and get wet, if that is what God is asking you to do.

This may be the conclusion of these pages, but our hope is that it is just the beginning of hundreds of journeys in and around the river. If you have a journey you would like to share with us, please visit www.throughtheriverbook.com .

Many blessings on your journey.

enerous®
Mind

W hat would the world look like if everyone was a *generous mind?*

To help people answer this question, we formed Generous Mind LLC as a think tank devoted to shining a light on people's potential to share what they know with others.

So what is a *generous mind?* It is someone who does not keep what they know locked in their head but instead strives to share with those around them. A *generous mind* is not limited to authors, public speakers, and teachers. Instead, anyone with the courage to share what God has entrusted to them can be generous with their thoughts and impact lives around them.

This book is an example of three *generous minds* working together. Partnering with Dr. Paul Hiebert was a process of collaborating to communicate a concept in a new and fresh way, making it practical for daily living. We pray that this act of generosity will bless you in your journey of understanding truth.

To find out more about what it means to be a *generous mind* visit: www.generousmind.com.

NOTES

Preface: Lessons at the Water's Edge

1. Paul G. Hiebert, *Missiological Implications of Epistemological Shifts: Affirming Truth in a Modern/Postmodern World* (Harrisburg, PA: Trinity Press International, 1999).

Chapter 1: Three Communities along the River

1. Using the analogy of a river to discuss different views of truth comes from Peter Berger, cited on page 68 of Hiebert's *Missiological Implications*.
2. Larry Samovar, Richard Porter, and Edwin McDaniel, *Intercultural Communication: A Reader* (Belmont, CA: Thomson Wadsworth, 2006), 34.
3. Hiebert, *Missiological Implications*, 84.
4. *American Heritage Dictionary*, 4th ed. (Boston: Houghton Mifflin, 2000).
5. Paul G. Hiebert, in discussion with authors, June 24, 2006.
6. C. S. Lewis, *Studies in Words* (Cambridge: Cambridge University Press, 1967), 6.
7. Ibid.
8. Hiebert, *Missiological Implications*, 2.

9.   Herman Melville, "Letter, June 1, 1851, to Nathaniel Hawthorne" in
     Correspondence, The Writings of Herman Melville, vol. 14, ed. Lynn Horth
     (Chicago: Northwestern University Press, 1993).
10. Found in *Phillips' Book of Great Thoughts and Funny Sayings* by Bob
     Phillips (Carol Stream, IL: Tyndale, 1993), 62.
11. http://www.worldofquotes.com/author/Winston-Churchill/1/index.
     html.

Chapter 2: The River Town Story

1.   *The Cambridge History of Philosophy, 1870–1945*, ed. Thomas Baldwin
     (Cambridge, UK: Cambridge University Press, 2003), 321.
2.   John Guest, *In Search of Certainty* (Ventura, CA: Regal Books, 1983),
     33.
3.   Hiebert, *Missiological Implications*, 112.
4.   Erwin Fahlbusch, Geoffrey Bromiley, Jan Milic Lochman, John Mbiti,
     and David Barrett, *The Encyclopedia of Christianity, Vol. 4* (Grand
     Rapids, MI: Eerdmans, 2005), 906.
5.   Thomas S. Kuhn, *The Copernican Revolution: Planetary Astronomy in the
     Development of Western Thought* (Cambridge, MA: Harvard University
     Press, 1992), 1.
6.   Ibid., 2.
7.   Hiebert, *Missiological Implications*, 43.
8.   Wilf Hey, "Albert Einstein: Father of Relativity Not Relativism,"
     Vision, http://www.vision.org/visionmedia/article.aspx?id=596
     (accessed April 29, 2008).
9.   Thomas Friedman, *The World Is Flat* (New York: Farrar, Straus &
     Giroux, 2005), 7.
10. http://en.wikipedia.org/wiki/Michael_Polanyi.
11. Hiebert, *Missiological Implications*, 74.
12. Charles Pierce, *Philosophical Writings of Pierce*, ed. Justice Buchler
     (Mineola, NY: Dover Publications, 1955), 18.

Chapter 3: Positivism

1.   Hiebert, *Missiological Implications*, 1.
2.   Ibid., 4–5.
3.   Ibid., 8.
4.   Ibid., 11–2
5.   David Harvey, *The Condition of Postmodernity: An Inquiry into the Origins
     of Cultural Change* (Malden, MA: Wiley-Blackwell, 1991), 12.
6.   Hiebert, *Missiological Implications*, 6.

7. Ibid., 10.
8. Ibid., 11.
9. Ibid., 6.
10. Ibid.
11. Ibid., 15.
12. Ibid., 13.
13. Ibid., 12.
14. Ibid., 13.
15. Ibid., 6.
16. Ibid., 22.
17. Ibid., 17.
18. Ibid., 22.
19. Ibid., 23.
20. Ibid., 22.
21. Ibid., 23.
22. Ibid., 19.
23. Ibid., 22.
24. Ibid., 19.
25. Ibid., 20.

Chapter 4: Instrumentalism

1. Hiebert, *Missiological Implications*, 39.
2. Ibid., 40.
3. Ibid., 41.
4. Ibid., 56.
5. Ibid., 45.
6. Ibid., 42.
7. Ibid., 43–4.
8. Ibid., 45.
9. Ibid.
10. Paul G. Hiebert, in discussion with authors, June 24, 2006.
11. Hiebert, *Missiological Implications*, 44.
12. Ibid., 54.
13. Ibid.
14. Ibid.
15. Ibid.
16. C. S. Lewis, *Studies in Words* (Cambridge, UK: Cambridge University Press, 1967), 7.
17. Hiebert, *Missiological Implications*, 53.
18. Ibid., 54.
19. Ibid., 68.
20. Ibid., 70.

21. Ibid., 60.
22. Ibid., 58.
23. Ibid., 57.

Chapter 5: Critical Realism

1. Hiebert, *Missiological Implications*, 74.
2. Hiebert, in discussion with authors, June 24, 2006.
3. Hiebert, *Missiological Implications*, 74.
4. Ibid., 69.
5. Ibid., 86.
6. Ibid., 92.
7. Ibid., 71–2.
8. Ibid., 124.
9. Ibid., 88–9.
10. Ibid., 77.
11. Ibid., 85.
12. Ibid., 77.
13. Ibid., 97.
14. Ibid., 94. The Jarvie quote is from his book *Rationality and Relativism: In Search of a Philosophy and History of Anthropology* (London: Routledge & Kegan Paul, 1984).
15. Ibid.
16. Ibid., 113.
17. Ibid., 102.
18. Ibid., 99.
19. Ibid., 102.
20. Ibid., 101.
21. Ibid.

Chapter 6: Experiencing Truth in Love

1. Matthew Henry, "The Complete Commentary on 1 Corinthians 13" in *Matthew Henry Complete Commentary on the Whole Bible*, 1706. http://www.studylight.org/com/mh-com/view.cgi?book=1co&chapter=013 (accessed April 29, 2008).
2. To understand the Greek words for *faith*, see: http://www.studylight.org/lex/grk/search.cgi?word=faith&search.x=18&search.y=13 (accessed April 29, 2008).
3. To understand the Greek words for *hope*, see: http://studylight.org/lex/grk/search.cgi?word=hope&search.x=16&search.y=10 (accessed April 29, 2008).

4. Adam Clarke, Commentary on John 8 in *The Adam Clarke Commentary*, 1832. http://www.studylight.org/com/acc/view.cgi?book=joh&chapter=008 (accessed April 29, 2008).

Chapter 7: Holding Truth Lenses Up to the Bible

1. Hiebert, *Missiological Implications*, 116.

Chapter 8: The Great Disturbance

1. Peter Kreeft, *The Journey* (Madison, WI: InterVarsity Press, 1996), 16.

Chapter 9: Truth Lenses and Relationships

1. Hiebert, *Missiological Implications*, 5.
2. Ibid., 14.
3. Ibid., 103.
4. Ibid.

Chapter 11: The World through Your Truth Lens

1. Hiebert, *Missiological Implications*, 27.
2. Ibid., 108.
3. Ibid., 28.
4. Ibid., 29.
5. Ibid., 63.
6. Ibid., 60.
7. Ibid., 62.
8. Ibid., 106
9. Ibid., 108.
10. Ibid., 114.
11. Ibid., 115.
12. Ibid., 109.

Chapter 12: Journeys through the River

1. Hiebert, *Missiological Implications*, 68.
2. Ibid., 1.
3. Ibid., xiv.